RIGHT IS MIGHT

RIGHT IS MIGHT

BY

RICHARD W. WETHERILL

HUMANETICS FELLOWSHIP ™

NOTE FROM THE PUBLISHER:

The manuscript for this book was written in 1950.

Because the author could not find a publisher willing to go out on a limb for honesty and right action during that period, the manuscript was filed away among his voluminous papers.

Since his death in 1989, the manuscript has been given careful editing. Some obviously dated material was eliminated, but the principles of right behavior that he put into words are ageless. They are all preserved.

Richard W. Wetherill, during his lifetime, was often described as a person who was scores of years ahead of his time. His associates and members of his research group think that his day has finally come. Increasingly it is becoming fashionable to be honest and right.

RIGHT IS MIGHT tells the reader how honesty and rightness are achieved in a person's private and public life. It also describes the exciting developments in the lives of persons who are applying the formula for successful living explained in the pages that follow.

Introduction

A Message of Optimism and Hope

M UCH IS right in the world, but also much is wrong. This
book is mostly concerned with what is wrong. It is not a
book of criticism and condemnation. It is one of explanation, optimism and hope. It promotes the doctrine that we,
as individuals, can save our world. It advocates procedures
with which each person can start by improving the satisfac-
tions and rewards of his own life.

Little is wrong in the world except what is caused by people's intentional or unintentional misdeeds. True, there are
occasional earthquakes, floods, windstorms or famine. But
the seasons go along in reasonably orderly succession, and
the vegetation renews itself each year without fail. That has
been true in the past, and although the pattern may change
at any time, it will presumably be true in the future. So it is
clear that nature is not the culprit. Most of everyone's suffering is caused by people. There is no use dodging that
basic fact.

This book rests on certain assumptions that are widely
accepted today. One of those assumptions is that society sadly
needs relief from the wrongs caused by men. Another is that
there cannot be the needed relief without a moral awaken-
ing that will open new channels of individual and mass
thought, leading to a gigantic swing in private and public
opinion. Another is that there must be reliable yardsticks
and procedures for diagnosing those ills, for prescribing

their cures, and for seeing that the cures are made effective. This book is one man's effort to define those yardsticks and procedures.

Doubtless what follows will include much that is unconventional. There is a reason for that. The reason is that the conventional procedures have not worked. They have led or allowed people to drift into what is now recognized as a critical and sorry estate. Even the modern and most advanced procedures have not stemmed the negative tide. The retrogression of recent years, in fact, suggests that many of those modern and most advanced procedures are negative in themselves.

First, if conventional procedures have not worked, what is needed is unconventional procedures. That necessarily means society needs procedures that are tried and proved effective but are not yet popular. It seems best to start with the problems that exist by reasoning first to their causes, then to their solutions. That is the approach that was used in the studies that led to this book.

Some readers may conclude that this book advocates a sort of idealism that may be impossible to achieve, but such is not the case. My dictionary defines idealism as "seeing things as they should be instead of as they are." That kind of idealism is necessary to check idealism against reality and note the differences. When you do that, what you get is the objective for a practical plan of action. To deride that use of idealism is to say that things should be as they are instead of as they should be, no matter how terribly wrong they are. By that line of reasoning, people excused feeding Christians to lions and sending Jews to death camps when it was fashionable.

Obviously the long-term trend of humanity has been toward improvement. The light of truth has burned brightly in occasional spots on this earth and may be burning brightly in unsuspected spots today. There have been many lost generations when, for the most part, that light had burned dimly at best. We should not let this present generation become one of those that is lost.

Many persons think that present predicaments demand a mental and emotional housecleaning all over the earth. We need a new system of reasoning that is different from what we have had. At least, we need new tools of reasoning that will change the answers we get in dealing with a considerable proportion of our basic problems.

To accomplish that, human nature being what it is, we must also make certain that using those tools does not involve self-sacrifice on the part of those persons who use them. Few persons have demonstrated any willingness to advance humanity while retarding themselves, even when there is ultimate personal gain to be had as a result. Therefore, we need tools that will benefit the individual user before they benefit humanity as a whole. This book will undertake the task of supplying those tools.

Some of those tools may seem utterly new, but, in reality, there is little that is new about them. Nevertheless, in combination, they provide a set of keys that will unlock the deep, rich secrets of an enlightened life for every person who seriously uses them.

Many persons will doubtless recognize in those tools the framework of a formula that is almost as old as recorded history. Some of our sages have put portions of that formula into words. Religious writings are filled with such words. I feel that the formula represents what every enlightened person has long desired to say and will be glad it is at last being said.

Occasional enlightened persons will say that the basic tenets of that formula are so simple they are hardly worth mentioning. Except for the fact that they are so generally disregarded, that may be so. But perhaps we have got ourselves into trouble because so many have forsaken the obvious. Clearly, if that is true, the obvious must be retold to humanity.

In searching for a formula that will solve people's basic problems, we must find one that combines workability with simplicity.

Often it is said that life has become too complicated to understand. It is not life that has become complicated, but rather, the mechanisms of life. Almost every new push-button device introduces new simplicity into the process of living. So we normally leave the technicalities behind those push-buttons to the experts who devise, produce and service them. If we don't get simpler living as a result, that is our fault.

Perhaps it is true that our social problems have become too complicated for the layman to understand. But experience has taught that, thus far, the experts have not acquired sufficient ability that we can entrust them with our social problems as we do our problems of electronic and mechanical devices.

An amateur social planner may feel that he can outdo the professionals, and, in important respects, he can. It is only an occasional person who thinks he can fix his own television set better than an expert. Part of the reason may be that the amateur social planner detects flaws in the work of the experts, whereas the TV repairman quickly proves that he knows what he is doing.

This book is not intended to be hard on the experts. We all recognize, as especially do they, that the social sciences have lagged far behind the physical sciences in the amount of research given them and in the results that research has disclosed. One reason is that a person cannot patent and directly profit by the results of social research as he can in the electronic, mechanical, chemical and other physical fields. Consequently there is less incentive to support and conduct effective social research programs. Another reason is that most of our research techniques were developed essentially to permit physical studies, and many of the basic research methods are ill-adapted to nonphysical studies. There are other important reasons that cannot be given direct attention here.

Clearly we need a vast simplification of today's broad social problems as faced by the average person if we expect to resolve them.

The right formula will be seen to involve procedures that let people go on working and amusing themselves as they do now. It will, however, change their manner of working and playing. It will enrich their personal lives and, therefore, will be attractive to them. At the same time, it will get people out of the dilemmas that threaten to engulf them.

I repeat, a purpose of this book is to supply that formula.

It cannot be described briefly, but I have tried to waste no words. The formula cannot be put into capsules and sold in the manner of popular drugs. It must be read and digested. Once a person grasps the formula, it is hard to imagine that he will fail to start putting it to work. He will start having more opportunities, more rationality and more freedom from trouble. He will be the first to benefit. His success will be in proportion to his making the formula work, and it will work if those things he craves are right.

Preparation of this book has involved certain troubles with our language. Many abstract words are used that often mean different things to different people. Moreover, our common nontechnical language contains no word to express an exact meaning that is required. Sometimes that necessitates detailed explanations to make intended meanings clear. In grasping those meanings, the common dictionary definition rather than a specialized technical usage should always be assumed.

There is only one problem that proved so difficult to solve that special explanation is required.

Repeatedly this book uses the term "average person." That term is in disrepute, because it represents a statistical image that has no counterpart in real life. But it is a convenient term if its meaning is understood as intended. There seems no recourse except to say that it is used in the general connotation of an earlier day. It signifies the middle one-third of our population who most nearly approximate what is average in relation to the quality under discussion. When that quality is negative, as is a specific form of dishonesty, the quality will be considered common to both the middle and lower thirds of our population. When it is positive, as is a specific form of honesty, the quality will be considered common to both the middle and upper thirds. In either case, the boundaries represent only a rough approximation. Thus, in every case, the term will ascribe a quality to roughly two-thirds of our population—important because they constitute a working majority who can do much to control society's destiny. The term average person is still a statistical monstrosity, but defining and using it in the foregoing sense will save confusion later on.

Contents

Chapter 1

Right Will Eventually Prevail

IT IS no secret that the world is in trouble. People don't need to be told that there is nefarious plotting among nations, that governments are infested with graft and corruption, that business and industry are honeycombed with sharp practices, and that all too many individuals are out for themselves first, last, and all the time—to the detriment of others. Nor do people need to be told that they face many serious environmental problems and dilemmas that are not being resolved.

Too few people recognize any connection between their wrongs and the troubles they cause.

Among all the lessons taught by history, the most important is that the forces of right ultimately triumph in every long-continued struggle. The forces of wrong are doomed to ultimate extinction, as is evident in the lives of every past oppressor and tyrant who ever trod this earth.

A person needs to be afraid only to the extent that he is wrong. People instinctively know it—at least people who are not blinded by cupidity, excessive ambition or other destructive drives.

Just as would-be conquerors have striven to gain control by aggressive action, so have innumerable men and women chosen dishonest, immoral shortcuts to their objectives, trying to stack the cards in their favor in the game of life. But right has a way of ultimately succeeding as well as a definite short-term and immediate value. The easiest way to gain true advantage is to be right.

This book will advance and pursue the thesis that most of society's serious problems and dilemmas have arisen from persistent wrongs practiced by a majority of people. It will not be concerned with the rights and wrongs of smoking, drinking, gambling or sex; it will seldom deal with fine distinctions of any sort. Instead, it will deal with the sort of wrongs that virtually every unbiased and objective observer would agree at once are both wrong and indefensible.

It will show that behind almost every wrong there are one or more persons who caused and support it. It will show that almost every wrong is an expression of intentional or unintentional dishonesty on the part of those persons who caused and support it. It will show that masses of people are dishonest, both individually and collectively, and that there is dishonesty on virtually every level of society. It will show that society needs to practice fundamental honesty in its activities as a prelude to revolutionizing human thought. It will show that until people establish their thinking on a new plane of honesty their basic problems cannot be solved.

It will be established that honesty is the way to correct our human problems and that there is no other.

Thus this book will pinpoint the exact nature of a delusion that has captured the minds of billions of people, some who think there is nothing amiss and others who know that something is amiss but do not know what causes their fear and frustration. It will explain how to correct delusions people do not know they have. It will demonstrate that the result will not only be the elimination of trouble but also the opening of hitherto unsuspected horizons of spectacular opportunity. It will describe the tools needed to spread the good word everywhere.

If you believe in honesty not merely as an ideal but as a daily reality, you are going to like this book. If you believe that it is wrong to lie, steal, cheat, neglect your responsibilities or hurt your fellow men, this book contains no basic assertion you will resent. But if you are like the average person, you had better prepare yourself for a few shocks. At first, some of those shocks may be unsettling. Have the courage to look facts in the face. If you do, you are going to get several interesting and profitable surprises.

Clearly, I am dealing with a touchy subject. If you want to know how touchy it is, select almost any person you know and accuse him of being dishonest.

I am going to show that the majority of people are habitually dishonest in several unnoticed but important ways. I am going to show that many are dishonest on purpose for selfish gain and others for reasons they consider little short of holy. And I am going to show that those who are dishonest only for what they consider good reasons are just as dishonest and detrimental to human welfare as those who are dishonest only for selfish gain.

For a person keenly conscious of his own past mistakes, it has taken courage to make the assertions you have been reading and more courage to make the assertions to come. But be assured that I do not feel cocky about them, because I learned what happens when you make mistakes by the simple process of making them. Sometimes I think I have learned from almost every mistake that a person can make, and often it has taken more than one repetition to make the lesson clear. Nevertheless, I have determined to write about what I have learned.

When certain individuals read these pages, they may be reminded of the scriptural injunction, "Let him who is without sin cast the first stone." I don't propose to cast any stones, but I do propose to tell the truth.

If Diogenes were here with his lantern today, I think he would find as few honest people as he found in ancient Greece.

In the twenty-three centuries since Diogenes, people have made great progress in dealing with physical things. They have learned to collect innumerable natural resources and convert them for human use. They have given the public all manner of products and devices—even developed a nuclear arsenal. Most of the progress has occurred in the physical realm while in the nonphysical realm, the rate of development is much less significant. Most people have not even solved the problems of ordinary dealings with one another, but as many people are saying, we had better solve them if we intend to survive.

That people may be able to solve them, there is considerable hope. To do it, what is most urgently needed is a greater proportion of incorruptible people. As those incorruptible people gain influence, everybody's troubles will diminish. And when the facts get abroad, incorruptible people are likely to turn up on all sides. There are good reasons for expecting that to happen.

Most persons would agree that every individual wrong is likely to be detrimental to society as a whole and that a world in which individual good damages the common good does not make sense. This book will make clear that every wrong is detrimental to the individual who causes and supports it. It will make clear that resort to widespread honesty will bring most of the universal troubles to an abrupt halt. More important, it will make clear that resort to honesty on the part of one individual anywhere will do much to stop trouble for him, without regard to what is done by others whom he cannot influence or control. There is just one sort of person for whom that will not be true. He is a person whose wrongs have already done irrevocable damage from which he cannot escape.

It cannot be denied that there is great evil occurring in the world. Examples of obvious wrong are publicized every day, on every level of society everywhere. To miss seeing those wrongs, a person would have to close his eyes to most current events. That is a sad commentary on human affairs, but people may as well face the facts. Otherwise their minds are certain to be thrown off the paths of logic, and no more time should be wasted in confusion.

The average person (by average person I mean the majority of all persons*) has made so many compromises with his personal integrity that he hardly knows what real integrity is. So persistent have people's dishonest habits become that they usually go unrecognized. They have become embodied in our systems of public, private and business life.

There is no need to name specific people. It is enough to define the four general groups that people fall into: 1. Those who like and grow fat on an existing devious system. (This book will show that they are not so fortunate as they assume.) 2. Those who feel caught in the system's vicious toils and consider it practical to go along. (When the system is changed, they'll heave a sigh of relief.) 3. Those who have broad moral scruples and try not to compromise them. (They represent vital landmarks pointing to a better world.) 4. Those who are too blind to know what is going on. (Often they give their support to members of the first group.) Whether a person likes it or not, that is the situation; and the evidence is that the first group, the dishonest element, is in the ascendant.

Now that I have left no doubt regarding my opinion of society's mass depravity, let us turn to another side of the picture.

Perhaps you noticed that the foregoing information is

---

*See definition of average person in the Introduction.

presented quite dispassionately. Customarily displays of dishonesty and wrong are denounced indignantly. But indignation serves no useful purpose. As will be shown, it is only another form of wrong. In addition, the person who is wrong is in trouble. He needs help. He needs it a great deal more than he needs condemnation and criticism.

It is not rational to imagine that a person would purposefully get himself into trouble. That would be like a person's banging his head against a stone wall in the belief that such conduct improves his well-being. When a person understands why people get into trouble, it generates more sympathy than bitterness and makes him feel inclined toward help rather than recrimination.

There are no bad people. There are only people who make bad mistakes.

Many of those who cause our most serious troubles are really well-meaning individuals who are quite unintentionally dishonest in ways they do not suspect. Some are knowingly dishonest in ways that they justify by means of rationalizations and noble motives. It is true that there are others who, without conscience, are out for themselves; but it all adds up to the same result. They are making trouble for themselves and for others. When they understand what they are doing, they will stop. I am optimistic enough to think that the change will come in the present generation. Certainly it is not too much to hope that we can reverse the trend.

There are a thousand concepts I should like to present all at once, but they will have to be presented in sequence.

What I am trying to do is to build a case that should alter the mass thinking of the human race, and to do that, it is necessary to proceed in small steps. It causes me to make various statements that, at first, a person may be inclined to challenge, but there is no other way. If he follows the steps laid out in this book, he will perceive the path to a better life.

Some persons may think I am expecting too much. It must be admitted that altering the mass thinking of the human race will take a bit of doing, and to accomplish it, I will need a great deal of help from the people who thoughtfully read this book. As they understand, I predict their help will be wholehearted and enthusiastic.

In addition to those who read this book, there are many individuals who, in their own way, have made substantial contributions to the general movement of which this book will become a part. There are leaders and writers who are both vocal and articulate in advancing the cause of right. Usually their remarks are tied in with specific topics relating to problems that have been mishandled. Often they are just as outspoken as I. They should be pleased to learn that the basic component of all problems is being presented so that solution for antisocial behavior of all kinds can be made known.

This book is not for everybody. There are plenty of people who will not read it. There are some who will read a few pages and toss the book aside. There are others who will read straight through what most directly applies to them without realizing the connection. But I think there will be enough who digest its contents and put those contents to practical use. They will apply what they learn in their own lives and be better off for it. Many of them will exert influence in the lives of others and thus spread improvement far afield.

If there are just ten thousand of those people, that would be enough to start a movement that could change the world. In the process, their sort of thinking would gain control of the world's business. That would benefit everyone. But it would benefit the ten thousand people first.

I count on a vast amount of help from women, because many of them are in a position to influence at least one man. That they will do it in many cases, I have no doubt. A woman could hardly find a surer way of getting her husband or male friends advanced in their careers and earnings. Thus she can combine a moral crusade with practical considerations—and benefit in both respects.

I also expect much help from the younger generation, although it will doubtless take time for their influence to make itself impressive. There are two reasons why their help is vital. One, their minds are not as cluttered by misinformation and prejudice that must be corrected and dislodged. The other reason is that soon they will be running our affairs.

A few associates advised me, "Write to the person with a ten-year-old mind. He is the person you must persuade." That approach could not be right. The person with a ten-year-old mind is not reached by writing to him. Nor can I simplify a complicated presentation to suit his powers of absorption. But that is an academic matter, because the average ten-year-old can't or won't read anything important or serious even if put into his hand.

After eliminating the people who can't or won't read anything serious and important, there are perhaps twenty-five per cent of the population left—unless I am too optimistic. That group contains the people of influence who set much of the pattern for what is accepted by others. The bulk of the job must be done through them if it is to be done at all. As movement toward right thinking gains momentum, that influential group will be infused with ideas and plans of approach that will make their influence effective.

By practical experience, I have learned that the lowest worker in the economic scale (including the person who reads least) is receptive to these ideas when skillfully presented. I have learned that he is often more quickly receptive than the person of greater emotional and intellectual maturity. He will usually not be a problem so long as there is someone willing and able to talk to him. That I can say with the voice of experience. Techniques of dealing with those persons will be embodied in chapters to come, affording help to teachers, clergymen, business and industrial executives, personnel managers and others in a position to make their leadership effective.

Often it is said that nobody can change human nature. Perhaps not, but we can change people's thinking, and through that, their behavior can be changed. For sufficient reason, their thinking can be changed almost at once—on a mass scale, too.

There are two ways to change people's thinking. One is by persuasion, and the other is by force. Force is not a suitable tool. I am reminded of the quotation "A man convinced against his will is of the same opinion still." There is a kind of force though that does get results. But first, I should like to discuss persuasion, because that is the basic approach of this book. The simplest kind of persuasion results from setting a good example. The person who does, thereby gives himself a better foundation for the stronger kinds of persuasion.

The purpose of persuasion is to induce voluntary action. Therefore, ***persuasion must offer attraction toward personal advantage and gain or toward the opportunity to avoid trouble and loss.*** When those rewards are held forth and the other person is convinced, directly or indirectly, that the action suggested will give them to him, he will surely cooperate.

Succeeding chapters will define the important rewards of honesty. Those rewards can briefly be indicated by saying that the person who understands and applies the principles described in this book will open unimagined opportunities. He will have a perfect formula for achievement and success. He will understand that right will eventually prevail.

Succeeding chapters will also define the penalties of dishonesty—even unintentional or so-called noble dishonesty. It could be said that the person who rejects this information will thus deny himself his best opportunity to grow and prosper. Such a person inevitably remains his own worst enemy. Only as he becomes convinced that he has reduced his effectiveness and that his troubles are mainly his own fault will he start seeking improvement.

Such are the available tools of persuasion. Properly used, they have almost the effect of force. By analogy, let me cite a practical example.

If you were standing on a railroad track and a friend were to shout, "A train is coming!" you would accept his word and get off. If the shout came from a stranger, you would probably still respond even though you had no basis for judging his veracity. But suppose you didn't know that you were standing on a track? You would instinctively look for the track and then for the train. When you saw them no matter who provided the warning, friend or foe, you would get off the track.

The victim of wrong thinking is in much that position. As the message unfolds, he will see the vision that can change his life, and he will seek that change.

Just in case you need it as badly as I did, I am going to shout, "A TRAIN IS COMING!" In effect, I am going to describe another place to jump to when the danger in which society is living is seen by the reader who realizes that there is no other choice. I will show how that danger generates a negative force that can be replaced by a dynamic positive force that can make him invulnerable, take the effort out of his exertions, and enable him to do what he wants to do—to the exclusion of what he does not want to do.

Earlier I promised to discuss how to change people's thinking by force.

The easy way to force a change in another person's thinking is to deprive him of a desired opportunity unless or until that change is made. Often that will force him to change through sheer economic necessity. It is a delicate procedure, both to avoid unfairness and to assure a successful outcome, and there are many ways to apply it. A person can withdraw his patronage from a store, withhold his vote from a candidate or refuse to carry out dishonest instructions of his employer. It is true that his action counts as only one factor, but it is surprising how often that factor is decisive.

Much dishonesty succeeds only because it is supported and protected by people in surrounding positions. Only mass dishonesty could perpetuate many of those situations, and some of them will be easy to break up by use of honest techniques to be described. Within any group, you need convert only enough people to alter the balance of power, and it is usually easy to gain recruits for any clearly stated, sound moral cause. There are situations in which nobody's decision is valid except your own. That is the case when the other fellow wants an advantage or opportunity that only you are in a position to withhold or provide.

Another way to force a change is to start direct competition with the dishonest person. When that competition is made effective, the result will be one of two things: either the dishonest person will change his thinking, or he will be replaced. In many practical situations, the implication of force is clear.

Whether the average person has ever considered it, it is far easier to compete successfully with the person who is on the wrong track than with the person who is not—provided you are on the right track yourself. Besides when a person gets the habit of doing it that way, he discovers that direct competition, even in a capitalist economy, is no longer a necessary part of success. All right purposes can be served without it.

The person likely to resist that approach, it seems to me, is one who has convictions for which he has repeatedly gone on record. Perhaps he has interests to protect. In such a case, he may be almost irrevocably prejudiced against the logic herein employed.

We can hope only to surround the prejudiced person with patterns of influence and example that will demonstrate a better way of life. If need be, influence and example can be supplemented with stronger devices such as withdrawal of support. When a large number of persons actually participate in a movement of that sort, whether organized or spontaneous, those who refuse to change will inevitably ensure their own downfall.

It will be demonstrated that no aggressive action is needed to secure a victory for the forces of right. And in the meantime, those who have provided the patterns of good influence and example will find that their lives have flowered as a result. They will have demonstrated that *right will eventually prevail as the eternal basis of might.*

Chapter 2

Infallible Behavioral Formula

SHORTLY AFTER my initiation into the fraternity of those who must work for a living, I made the disappointing discovery that I and nearly all people were slaves: to habit, convention, governmental demands, employers. But above all, people were slaves to the need for a source of continuing income. What is said and done, in large measure, is dictated by that need. It was a little like discovering I was an anteater and could not get a meal except by grubbing in the dirt. It didn't seem right.

I wanted freedom from such slavery. So I started looking for someone who had turned the trick. I didn't find him. Lacking opportunity to copy a successful practitioner, I decided to strike out for myself. At first, I got into a certain amount of confusion, but as a result, I also learned how to be free by embracing a surprisingly simple concept.

If you make up your mind to it, you can do what you want to do, and you can do it to the exclusion of doing what you don't want to do.

It has been many years since I first phrased that concept. To say that I have lived by it ever since would not be truthful, but I have come a great deal closer to it than you might expect. The effort to do it led to an astonishing sequence of discoveries.

One of the first discoveries was that there are strings attached to the concept. A person cannot constitute himself

15

or herself sole arbiter of his destiny without regard for the consequences of his behavior in the lives of others. I am not referring to legal entanglements. I am talking about entanglements that are essentially moral, and why it is necessary to avoid them.

Avoiding moral entanglements, it turned out, puts no restrictions on anybody's freedom. Instead, the techniques of avoiding moral entanglements are exactly the techniques that make genuine freedom possible. Those techniques are embodied in a simple formula that I gradually learned to use, and its implications go far beyond the welfare of the individual. To apply that formula, you need common sense rather than unquestioning faith.

When you turn the switch that feeds power to a light bulb, it goes on. You don't have to understand what you are doing, you don't have to know anything about electricity, you don't have to have faith in the result. The light goes on nevertheless. You take the result for granted because you have seen it happen so often. Besides, you know you get the same result if you turn the switch by accident. You don't get conceited over your prowess in producing light, because you know that a monkey could turn the switch and get the same result. Your only advantage over the monkey, perhaps, is that you know the location of the switch and what it is for.

In the next pages, I am going to locate a switch that will produce enlightenment and give you the advantages that are presently benefiting only a fortunate few.

It has often been said that on this earth there is all that is needed to enjoy a veritable Garden of Eden, where people could live replete with happiness and freedom from want. That is true. There is an easily mastered formula by which so fortunate an estate could be achieved, and it is the formula we are about to discuss. The wonder is that so many centuries have passed while mankind has neglected to bring that formula into focus and see it for what it is.

The safety of everybody depends on adoption of that formula by the masses. That may be hard to induce. But whether it is finally induced or not, the average person can create a private Garden of Eden, replete with happiness and freedom from want. The formula is the key.

Only by adopting that formula can the individual make himself free and invulnerable. Only thus does a person make a proper contribution to freedom and invulnerability for society as a whole. In other words, by opening the door to abundance for himself, he also opens the door—if only a crack—to abundance for all other fellow beings.

Do not be surprised that the formula is simple, for simplicity is a natural characteristic of every basic concept that has motivated humanity.

Here are the words of the formula that can transform your life: ***Always think, say and do what is right. Refuse to think, say or do what is wrong.***

To a certain few people, that formula comes as no surprise. And I'll tell you something about those people. In a world filled with conflict and tribulation, those people function calmly. They aren't seeking peace of mind because they have it. Nor does it resemble a quiet somnolence that comes from ignoring the troubles of society and pretending that all's well with the world. Those people are realists. They know what is going wrong, and they are doing something constructive about it. They want to act instead of relax; they want to work instead of play; they want to meet life head on because their skills, energies and ingenuity are constantly challenged by the opportunities and events of life.

There is something else about those people. They are doing exactly what they want to do. No vocational troubles plague them. Whatever they attempt works out. Their lives open before them and present them with every opportunity they need. They never have to serve contradictory purposes or interests, never have to be two places at once, never suffer from anxiety or depression—not while living in accord with that formula.

But tell that formula to the average person, and you may be rebuffed.

At once, a dozen objections are likely to tumble forth. "But I always do the right thing," one may say. He does? Then he is different from almost any person I have ever met. As a matter of sober fact, I am not sure that I know anybody who can clearly distinguish between right and wrong in all decisions. Why that is, I shall discuss in chapters to come. In the light of that knowledge, I shall explain exactly what a person has to do to develop the ability to make unerring right choices.

"Sometimes it doesn't pay to do the right thing," another may say. The simple fact is that doing the right thing always pays, and that the only way to get into trouble is to do the wrong thing. The statement that wrong action can lead to right results, or that right action can lead to wrong results is a contradiction in terms, although it is true that right action handled in a wrong way can cause trouble because an element of wrong was introduced.

To say that it doesn't pay to do the right thing is to say that right is not expedient. That is untrue. Except under a common distortion of thought, the terms right and expedient are identical in meaning. The reason there are two words to describe the same concept is that so many persons are unaware of the truth. For it is a truth that is known only to persons who are spiritually enlightened, and it is a truth everybody should learn.

There will be skeptics who dispute the basic assertion

that literal right is always expedient. Those skeptics tend to pride themselves on their intelligence and on their application of logic to all their problems. The next point should give them pause.

The value of logic is that it affords a system of exact reasoning. Perhaps the most widely understood device of logic is the syllogism: All men are mortal; I am a man; therefore, I am mortal. Here is a syllogism that puts my point across: What is right, according to William James is what works; what works, according to the dictionary, is expedient; therefore what is right is expedient.

Who dares to say that right is wrong? Who could deny that right is expedient? I have met people who have done both. Logical reasoning, I have learned by experience, is not enough to satisfy dissenters to truth. They labor the question interminably, often in resentment and sometimes in outright anger. Yet some of those people have great influence, and in proportion to their influence, they are a threat to society's welfare.

When logic leads those people into a trap that refutes their preconceived notions, they forsake logic and resort to emotion. They are reluctant to accept what they have never considered, because it is inconsistent with many misguided events of their past. Have they no confidence in logic, the science of exact reasoning? Have they more confidence in the prejudiced promptings of their emotions? Unfortunately, they have!

Even in the commonest parlance, what is not expedient is wrong. It cannot work, so it cannot be right. Therefore, only what is expedient is right. In any parlance, only what is expedient can work. If it works, it cannot be wrong. Therefore, only what is expedient is right. Thus we come out with the same conclusions: ***What is right cannot be inexpedient or wrong.***

A dozen past compromises with right may spring to the

mind of any reasonably honest person. All logic to the contrary, he considers those compromises to be expedient. How can he justify them? It is not enough to say that he cannot. He may insist on his point despite all the contradictions of logic, so he must be given no room for doubt. If possible, he must be convinced. In view of the history of human affairs, that may not be easy—even though he knows that the basic tenets of our broad social policies have brought human affairs to their present sorry estate.

Always do the right thing. Right action leads to right results. Wrong action leads to wrong results. Right action cannot lead to wrong results. Wrong action cannot lead to right results. Right can never contradict proper duty; all are identical by definition.

These statements are clear and distinct, inarguable and obvious; it is strange that any person would question them.

Here I should like to say why I have emphasized the establishment of what most people instinctively know. If you are puzzled that I have so heavily stressed the identity between right and expediency, let me explain why.

For many years I have been bursting with the ideas that fill these pages and have discussed them with a wide variety of people. Most of them have resentfully disagreed that right is always expedient. On no other subject have I encountered such frequent and serious skepticism.

There are many who have rejected the truth in the past, are rejecting it today and, unless we put a stop to their folly, will reject it in the future—to our cost as well as theirs.

Occasionally, however, I discovered somebody who raised his eyebrows in surprise that the point should be expressed at all. "I thought everybody knew that," he would say. "Why all the fuss about anything so obvious?"

The sharp distinction between the two groups, at first,

was puzzling. But those who agreed provided stimulation, while those who didn't provided a challenge. The stimulation kept me on the job, and the challenge taught me the arguments that must be met. Point by point, I have learned the objections so that today I think I can answer them all.

In recent years I have tested the answers by trying them on the skeptics, and those skeptics are just as prevalent now as when I started. But there is a big difference. The skeptics do not remain skeptical. Instead, they say, "I hope you get that story across. It's exactly what this sick society needs."

Of course, there are some who will resist the whole philosophy of these pages. I do not envy them the positions they must take to make their arguments appear convincing or even to state them. In effect, those people must work from the assumptions that wrong is right and that right is wrong. That is as impossible as proving that up is down. Their hair-splitting ingenuity may capture temporary adherents, but their logic is specious and cannot endure.

Many persons may have to condition their thinking before they can accept all that follows. But there is evidence that the only person who will reject the basic tenets is the one who consciously thinks it is expedient and profitable to do what is wrong and has adopted a policy to that effect.

If such people there be, their howls may go up to heaven, but those howls will be aimed in the wrong direction. So, perhaps, will be the people who utter them unless they mend their ways.

There may be skeptics, but nobody can justify wrong to an intelligent listener except when that listener is a fellow conspirator. The case for right stands up under the most rigorous and logical analysis. To present that case demands no oversimplification of a complicated set of ideals hedged in by if's, and's, and but's. The presentation is based on irrefutable truth. Adoption of any opposite assumption as the basis of action is crime against humanity. Only because that crime is so perpetually committed have human affairs come to their present perilous state.

Skeptics there may be, but the day will come when it is realized that the principle of absolute right is the crux of man's relation to man, and also of man's relation to God.

At the time of this publication, it may be difficult to recognize the person who espouses absolute right. He seldom talks about it. He has learned that people who hear his theories expounded silently accuse him of claims to saintliness and judge him critically. He has learned people seldom realize his behavior is controlled by recognition of a natural law. Instead they may decide he is trying to get away with something.

It is a popular condemnation of the literal moralist that he "sees the world in black and white; to him there are no grays." Recognize that gray is compounded of black and white, and the comparison becomes more valid.

Let us return to our consideration of the objections that arise when the formula for successful living is put into words.

"Right and wrong are relative qualities," someone may say. "One thing is more right but less wrong than another. Often a thing is partly wrong and partly right. There is seldom a clear-cut distinction."

Under analysis a person discovers that situations consist of elements, some of which are wrong and others right. If he sorts out and examines those elements, truth is easily separated from error. Some tasks of sorting are more difficult than others, but only because they are more complicated. They have more elements; therefore, they take more time to analyze, or perhaps the individual lacks knowledge of how to deal with them.

Often it is hard to collect all the pertinent facts. Some

facts must be filled in by speculation, and here it is important that the speculation be done by a scrupulous person. If those analyses are continued long enough, there finally emerges a clear pattern of distinctions between right and wrong. Those who act before a clear pattern emerges are the persons whose irresponsibility is causing much of society's trouble.

There are other characteristic objections, and there is an answer to each. "What is right is what is generally sanctioned." If approval is the criterion, moral values could be fixed by flexible whims. "What is right is determined by custom." If we are to judge right by what people do, there would be no point in seeking improvement. "Right depends on your viewpoint and interests." If that were true, the end justifies the means. "What is right in this place will be wrong in another." Then do it here but not there. "What is right today will be wrong tomorrow." Then do it today only. "What is right for one person will be wrong for another." Let him do it for whom it is right but not for others.

Such are the comments that have greeted the simple formula: *Always think, say, and do what is right. Refuse to think, say, or do what is wrong.* People who make those comments are living in clouds of delusion. Right is clear and distinct. It is a positive quality. There is no such thing as an indefinite dividing line. There are only people who do not perceive the truth, and that is why humanity does not have a Garden of Eden today.

As children, all of us learned to handle the problems of ordinary arithmetic. There are vital lessons in arithmetic that we generally overlook. First, the easy way to solve a problem necessitates breaking it down into its simple and obvious steps. Second, each step constitutes a minor problem in itself to which there is an easy answer. Third, when you put together the right answers to the minor problems, you get the right answer to the problem as a whole. The procedure can be proved by adding a column of figures; every competent person who adds the same column gets exactly the same answer.

In handling the more complicated problems of life, people often are too negligent to be thorough. They use slipshod methods that leave too much to the imagination. Instead of confining themselves to the facts, they let emotions creep in. They get answers they want rather than answers that are right. When someone challenges them, they feel obligated to prove the correctness of their decisions, quibbling and splitting hairs.

For the problem that is really broken down into its essential elements, the hair-splitting can be skipped, because every distinction between right and wrong becomes easy. It can be made by the person directly involved or by any observer in possession of the facts. In rational moments practically everybody realizes that.

If you want to experiment, select an adult at random and question his ability to tell right from wrong. If he isn't too angry to talk, he will give you a stiff argument.

The fact is that everybody has the ability to choose what is right, and he knows it. But it may also be true that he is often confused. In his confusion he may erect elaborate defenses for his wrong decisions. In effect, he may say to himself, "This is the time when it is right to do the wrong thing." The temptation to form such a concept should instantly show that he is off the track—provided he knows anything about logic.

I have introduced the word temptation on purpose, for every normal person can tell right from wrong except when temptation somehow undermines his reason. Let him learn to recognize and resist temptation. Let him learn the areas in which he is competent to make sound moral choices and then extend those areas. That will give him more freedom, because he won't get into trouble. But he should be given no more responsibility than his existing stage of moral maturity enables him to manage for the common good, especially if he becomes one of our elected officials. Then everybody will have more freedom.

Chapter 3

There Is Never an Exception

THE TOPIC really being discussed is the basic morality of society. People tend to think of morality as something connected with the rights and wrongs of sex, which may be part of the general theme, but **morality consists of recognizing and doing what is right and recognizing and refusing to do what is wrong.** Morality is often thought to be very complicated, but in reality, it is not.

Much of the average person's morality reflects what his parents and teachers taught him as a child. Some reflects his religious training. In my family that involved a Christian Sunday school and church. Many people are somehow prejudiced against the morality of scripture, but I have noticed that they are usually the ones who have spent the least time reading it. If it will comfort them, I didn't learn these points from scripture. I learned them from life. Only later did I find that the Bible apparently contains them all—which ought to comfort the others.

It is worth noting that thus far in this country neither Christianity nor any other religion is being practiced on a national scale. When it is practiced by individuals, they find it a source of infinite satisfaction and an excellent guide to behavior. By their conduct, those persons have raised our average standards of behavior.

At this writing, people seem inclined to regulate their lives by reference to surveys. For example, there is the Kinsey

Report, touted as a scientific treatise for the eyes of doctors, but advertised and sold in large volume to the general public. Many magazine articles and books were written about that report. The burden of the Report's findings seems to be that since people are sinful about sex perhaps our standards of behavior should be lowered to match what people actually do. That is an amazing reaction until you remember that there are multitudes of people who make no effort to distinguish between right and wrong.

Suppose the average person has sinned? Does that justify sin? Suppose the Kinsey Report had investigated stealing rather than sex behavior? What person could claim that he has never stolen, even once? Is the average person, therefore, a thief? Should we lower our standards to sanction thievery? By the same reasoning, should religion be discarded because it teaches a morality that few people practice?

What is needed is a realistic approach that is based on intelligent choices rather than on desire. People need to sharpen their ability to make distinctions between right and wrong and to do it from the facts of any given situation without reference to surveys that report what others do.

The question of how to separate right from wrong can be made very complicated, and it can also be simplified. It will be shown that most of life's problems are free from fine distinctions of any sort.

For example, consider the subject of truth. For all practical purposes, *a true statement is one in accord with the facts.* The answer to one plus one is two. Any other answer is wrong.

Now consider the matter of right and wrong as expressed in human behavior.

A little wrong is as wrong as a big wrong, because either wrong is absolutely wrong. In the field of human relations, for example, it is as wrong to chop off a man's finger without just cause as it is to chop off his head. It is as wrong to steal one cent as to steal a million dollars. One wrong may lead to more serious consequences than another and thus entail greater responsibility; nevertheless, any wrong is wrong. Follow the same reasoning a bit further, and put it in reverse. If it is wrong to chop off a man's head or his finger without just cause, the reason is that the act unjustly injures him. Therefore, it is as wrong (though less serious) to subtract from his happiness, to add to his misery, to injure his health, to reduce the esteem in which he is held by others, or even to cause him annoyance, again assuming that the action is taken without just cause. Moreover, a wrong caused by negligence is as wrong as one caused by intention.

Thus it is clear that people should not conduct themselves irresponsibly to the detriment of others. It is also clear, when a person measures the foregoing principles against the daily behavior of any randomly chosen persons, he finds that there are few of them who live in conformity with the principle of absolute right. When the mass of people learn of this principle and start guiding themselves by it, we will have a vastly better world.

The preceding chapter gave a formula that constitutes a virtually infallible rule of human behavior. That formula has a moral and religious aspect as well as one that is practical.

Nearly every civilized religion preaches some form of the Golden Rule, but religion too often is summed up in that precept: "Do unto others as you would have others do unto you." The same may be said of the whole problem of human relations. "Why read a book on how to succeed with people?" I have been asked. "When you have the Golden Rule, you have the whole thing."

Do you?

Without belittling one jot or tittle of that piece of scriptural guidance, I should like to suggest that Jesus had a great deal more to talk about than the Golden Rule. So did the Prophets. So does anyone who seriously addresses the subject today.

It might reasonably be said that the Golden Rule is a sort of abridged rule-of-thumb for everyday guidance of the person who cannot remember the other details. Even as such, it is often forgotten, and among those who do not forget, it is often abused.

Consider the following: "Did you consider it right to fix that man's traffic ticket?" I once asked a small-time politician. "Sure I did," he said. "It's just a matter of applying the Golden Rule. That's what I'd want him to do for me. Besides, it's practical. In a few weeks I'm going to want him to vote right. That's how we keep the party in power!"

Maybe that politician thought he was virtuous. Maybe he had his tongue in his cheek. Maybe he was just stupid. I don't know. But I do know he was not practicing the scriptural Golden Rule.

From the foregoing, it is evident that the Golden Rule is not an infallible guide to right behavior, at least, not by itself. But it is both implied and included in the deeper admonition: *think, say and do what is right; refuse to think, say and do what is wrong.* That admonition could keep a person out of troubles he never suspected he was in.

It would keep everybody out of trouble if everybody would properly apply it.

"Work on the politicians first," people say. But that evades a basic fact. The right place for every person to begin is with himself. He who does is the first to benefit. And now I am going to make several statements that need not be accepted because you assume that I am a reliable reporter, but because you see the reality of their correctness. There is one method by which to check: Apply to yourself the procedure I shall describe. Application provides the evidence—the reality.

Let us talk about several persons who were in trouble. We should recognize that trouble, especially serious trouble, is usually compounded of big and little wrongs and mistakes. Past offenses, provided they did not cause irrevocable damage, are less important than the wrongs and mistakes to come. They should be prevented. Each of those persons in trouble was given a formula. The conversation was something like this:

"There is a way out of your dilemma. You can find it in a surprisingly short time. Nobody can give it to you; you must find it for yourself. If you do what I ask you to do and refuse to do what I ask you to avoid, your life will start improving at once.

"Doubtless you will be astonished by the changes that will occur. Your problems will be solved. Your ills will be relieved. Your attitude will improve. Your energy and courage will grow and enable you to meet and master every task. Somehow life will start to organize itself. But don't take my word for it. Apply the formula, and judge for yourself.

"Whatever your aims in life, don't let them dominate your thinking. Let your mind be dominated by these words: *Think, say and do what is right. Refuse to think, say or do what is wrong.*"

When it is a person's intent to live by that formula if he is in doubt, he should take time to ponder. He should not act until he knows; then doubt will vanish. Events will open before him, his problems will work out, and his needs will be met. He will easily do what earlier seemed impossible, because any task done right is easy to perform. He will realize that fatigue, negative emotion, controversy and unrewarding struggle—such things as these—are signs of friction. They show that he is forcing his way against resistance.

Our conversation continued, "As a result of all this, you can expect a succession of events that look like miracles. You may not be able to connect a desirable result with its true cause and may recognize the cause only by the fact that no such miraculous happenings had previously occurred in your life. You may recognize the cause because I tell you that the same thing has already happened for others to whom I have given this same formula. For them, such happenings are now routine. They can be for you, too."

What sort of results? Those who needed money suddenly received it, usually from an unexpected source. Those who suffered from conflict and abuse at the hands of others found their relationships suddenly altered for the better. Those who couldn't sleep at night found rest. Those whose lives were tangled into complexities beyond belief discovered that their problems started untangling of their own accord, seemingly with little or no direct attention. I know of no person who did not get a spectacular result by faithfully applying the foregoing formula: *Think, say and do what is right; refuse to think, say or do what is wrong.*

The logic behind those examples will take time to unfold, but I shall describe a basic element of that logic for anyone whose skepticism demands immediate evidence. Consider a common situation faced by almost everybody.

Each person has a more or less conscious group of objectives that dominate his life, and they change from time to time. Persons who must earn a livelihood likely include among their objectives a desire to advance their careers. Often that becomes a person's dominating motive—held forth because society respects it. But what sins are committed in the name of that motive!

The person's definitions of right and wrong somehow base themselves on what advances or retards his or her career. At once, the person suffers a degree of moral blindness that blanks out part of his intelligence. The very faculty that must be used to chart a successful course and advance his career loses part of its usefulness. Automatically competitors become enemies, he compromises his conscience to suit an unprincipled superior, he seeks unfair advantages that will bring promotion, perhaps he shields the talents of others who may outshine him, and he may indulge in numerous other sharp practices often considered smart.

Those are some of the reasons why there are so many persons whose daily lives contradict the teachings of their religion, why so many persons have enemies, and why people fall into errors they cannot understand.

When a person suddenly develops the courage to face life honestly, even as an experiment, all those troubles start correcting themselves. A new light shines in his eyes, a new spring rises in his step, a new buoyancy results from the shedding of conscious and unconscious burdens. The rewards are beyond belief. Why? Because the right thing to do is the expedient thing to do. And a successful life free from trouble is the reward of right thinking and right action.

Of all the vital faculties available to man, the ability to base one's life on the principle of absolute right is the ability that underlies all the rest. The person who bases his life on that principle finds that all things are added unto him.

Always think, say and do the right thing.

That sentence is a thousand times more complicated than may seem evident at first. For twenty years it has been one of my basic pursuits to learn why people fall into error. As a result, I am convinced that what I have learned is of vital consequence to each and every person.

However, in another sense, that sentence is also a thousand times simpler than it may appear. While at times the ability to distinguish right from wrong may seem the most difficult of human virtues to acquire, it is easy to apply. Indeed, its application becomes quite natural and instinctive, effortless and exhilarating to the person who can cut through all the superficialities of a complicated life and decide, "Hereafter, I shall *intentionally* do what is right!"

Anyone who makes that decision—and means it—gets a series of additional surprises. So does everybody who knows him. Consider a specific situation.

Can you imagine yourself facing a crisis unlike any that you have previously encountered and yet find yourself responding instantly to what the occasion requires? If you think about it, you will realize that you have done precisely that, more than once.

What strange power came to your rescue? Surely not your education nor your experience. *Education is for what can be expected; experience is for what has happened before.* You didn't have time to think it through. You just had time to do the right thing. And, if you kept your head, you did it. Probably you didn't think much of the accomplishment then nor realize what had happened.

Despite any contradictory opinions, in a crisis, the individual is able to focus his attention onto the foundations of absolute right and solve the problem that confronts him. It happens on occasion to practically everybody. There is nothing strange or remarkable about it. What is strange is that people give so little recognition to this phenomenon. What is stranger is that this great power, so readily available in a crisis, is absent in our less crucial moments. There is a reason for that.

In a moment of crisis, one does not have time to plan. A person proceeds on instinct or not at all. In that moment of crisis, so long as one keeps his head, right thought and right action are almost synonymous. When there is time to calculate every move, all sorts of choices may arise.

Is it not true that what a person can do in a crisis he can also do when no crisis exists? What is there in a crisis to elevate his abilities to such heights?

It is evident that a crisis tends to draw on an individual's highest energies, give him strength, and produce a quick concentration of faculties. But it does more. Because it demands immediate action, it excludes a great deal of extraneous thought. It keeps him from exploring his fears and undermining his faith in himself and his capabilities. It keeps him from considering his selfish interests, seeing how he can squeeze the maximum profit out of his act, or otherwise confusing his inherent knowledge of what is right. It holds his faculties on the only consideration that counts—the consideration of what will resolve the crisis—what is right. And it makes him forget the extent to which society reveres education, experience, ambition and detailed planning. Not that there is anything wrong with those things when appropriate.

What all this means is that, in a crisis, the importance of right action becomes dominant. It dwarfs all other issues. And what this also means is that when no crisis exists, thought and action are too often conducted without the same foundation of safety. By our very opportunity to be thorough, we often defeat ourselves. We do it by forsaking our reference to absolute right.

How often have you gone through crucial situations that taxed you to the utmost? How often have you succeeded instinctively in doing the right thing? There is a feel to that experience, an emotional sensation not so much of moral rectitude as of safety and invulnerability. You can get that feel in every act of life. When you have it, no matter how great your problem, you will come through to success.

It would be foolhardy to suggest that you gain that feel by the process of confronting yourself with a series of crises just to test yourself. I discovered there is an artificiality about such testing that throws thinking off the track. Besides, there are enough crises in daily life to afford all the opportunity needed.

What is learned from meeting crises directly with a cool head and instinctive resort to right is that much of our daily planning is confusing and unnecessary.

Pursue that knowledge far enough, and a person discovers that he can enter almost any situation, however complicated, and quickly produce order. He can do it without advance planning and almost without effort. He discovers that often it is easier to do it than to refrain from doing it. That is an exciting piece of knowledge—perhaps the most exciting a person can possess.

Chapter 4

People Really Want To Be Right

IT IS a popular saying that the average person is honest. That saying is generally accepted and believed and passed along from one person to another as though it were true. I first heard it from a teacher who said, "Many people say that the average person is dishonest. Don't believe it. If you do, you will become a cynic. If you expect him to do the right thing, he usually will."

Of all my childhood lessons, that has been one of the most disastrous. For years I took it literally, and the story of what it cost is too long to tell here. I can say that it led me into two traps. One, I assumed that dishonest people were honest, which enabled them to delude me. Second, I adopted certain false standards, which had the effect of teaching me to do what I saw others doing who later proved to be dishonest.

I no longer believe that statement; it wasn't true thirty years ago, and it isn't true today.

Perhaps you think I have become the cynic my teacher predicted. No, I have confidence in the basic integrity of the average person. In a sense, he is just as honest as my teacher said; yet, in another sense, he is decidedly dishonest. You have to go very high on the ethical scale to find a person who lives by the principle of absolute right. The fact is that the average person is honest part of the time, is neither honest nor dishonest part of the time, and is dishonest the rest of the time.

What I realize today is that the average person has standards of conduct that he is not willing to violate, so there are certain dishonest acts that he will not perform. He will not pick your pocket. He will not rob your house. Perhaps he will not falsify his income tax return nor lie under oath.

He will not commit a dishonest offense that might land him in jail. But I am cynical enough to believe that fear of jail is not what deters him. There is something deeper.

The examples I have cited typify a string of offenses that are clearly against the law, because they are almost universally regarded as dishonest and detrimental to the general welfare. But the average person has more than fear of jail to consider. He knows that he has to get along with people and that he cannot unless he suits them reasonably well. He knows he cannot suit people if he disregards the almost universally accepted standards of decent behavior.

He will not risk conviction in a court of law, but neither will he knowingly risk conviction in the courts of public and private opinion. Therefore, he does not do what he knows his friends and associates strongly disapprove of, even though the act violates no formal law. I shall show that such standards give him much latitude in the direction of dishonesty and allow many dishonest policies to be practiced and advocated quite generally.

Fear of jail and of adverse public opinion seldom enter the average person's mind. He has other deterrents that work before those fears have a chance to surface. Those other deterrents are his own personal standards of behavior. Those standards may go an inch beyond the law or a mile, but whatever they are, they ordinarily determine what the average person does or does not do.

In a sense, fear of punishment under the law or at the hands of others is supplemented by fear of punishment of the wrongdoer by himself. That suggests a consideration of conscience.

By discreet questioning, I have learned that many adults do not seriously acknowledge a conscience. They call it a superstition inherited from forebears. But conscience is there, and it works. If you doubt it, just suppose no member of the human race had a conscience. What would life on this planet be like?

Conscience has been likened to an imaginary inner compass by which a person finds the direction he should travel, much as a pilot might steer his ship. However, that likeness does not really describe the conscience.

The person who follows his conscience knows that it is an instrument of infinite precision. In the opinion of its critics, apparently their primary objection is that it is not scientific. "The conscience cannot be relied on," said a scientist, "because its promptings are subjective." Then he excused himself, remarking that he was hungry, and he hurried out to lunch. I wonder how he knew?

Perhaps the lie detector affords the most objective scientific evidence that conscience really does exist. The lie detector measures physiological symptoms and translates them into evidence that can be read on a chart. It shows changes in such functions as respiration, perspiration and pulse rate. It verifies the great emotional burden a dishonest person must sustain. The burden springs out of the necessity to carry hidden lines of thought, representing the truth and his effort to conceal it. At the same time, he fabricates a spoken line of thought that is false. In the process his ingenuity is taxed, and he is burdened with fear. At the same time, his excitement is increased. The whole performance is met with emotional resistance. You can call that resistance anything you choose. I call it conscience.

Ordinarily conscience is not needed for deciding the proper direction of travel. Nor is it a device for choosing between right and wrong. Those functions belong to the brain.

I think conscience is an instrument for encouraging the person who knows what is right and wants to do it as well as an instrument for deterring or punishing the person who knows what is wrong but insists on doing it. And, because I hold that conscience is a vital human force, I am going to make the blunt assertion that ordinarily the average person does not invite the displeasure of his conscience by doing what he knows is really wrong. Neither does he do it by failing to do what he knows is really right. At least, not unless he is first placed under great temptation.

Temptation that is resisted strengthens character. Temptation that is not resisted erodes character. The person who ignores his conscience finds that over a period of time, it becomes desensitized—a characteristic malady of our age.

The person who has allowed his conscience to become desensitized needs nothing more urgently than to embark on a program to sensitize it again. That is not difficult. It consists of listening for the right inner promptings and attempting to respond to them no matter where they lead. I never met a person who said he got into trouble by that procedure, but I have met many persons who were afraid to try it.

In the foregoing, two functions of conscience were described, but there are more.

Conscience tells a person to do what he knows is right, and it also tells him not to do what he knows is wrong. The person who uses his brain to distinguish between right and wrong thus charts his path of action. Soon he discovers unexplainable occasions when his conscience exceeds the foregoing functions and actually furnishes a guiding impulse on its own account. The person who has learned to receive those impulses has an inspired guide for perfect motivation.

Anyone who does not know that should withhold passing judgment. I say that to give pause to the person who might otherwise persuade someone else to reject a correct idea. Rather than deride the truth, he would do well to start seeking and following inner guidance. After he starts doing that, he collects evidence that is convincing.

Medical therapists have described an emotional disease called overconscientiousness. It is not for me to say that there is no such disease, but some persons have used reports of it as justification for relaxing self-discipline. Before relaxing, there is some point in speculating. Taking your troubles more seriously than someone else thinks you should may indicate that nature has selected you for accomplishment. Isn't it true that a person perfects his performance only by trying to perfect his performance?

A person should not moderate the functioning of his conscience until he knows what he is doing.

Unless a person has an actual emotional disease, he should try giving his conscience complete freedom. He may discover that so-called overconscientiousness is nothing of the sort. The problem results from the individual's resistance to his inner promptings. Let him recognize and act on those promptings and resistance will subside. Simultaneously his life will flower and prosper.

Sometimes a person thinks the promptings of conscience are contradictory. That just indicates he has not learned to sort out right from wrong. The person whose employer insists that he violate his moral scruples, for example, cannot expect his conscience to accede. There is no contradiction of conscience no matter how a person may wrestle with himself. Under analysis, every such situation is found to have right on one side and temptation on the other.

In the early part of this chapter, I said that the average

person seldom knowingly risks punishment by others or himself. I discussed conscience sufficiently to show the bases of my reasoning. I showed that the average person wants to be right, that he wants it with good reason, and that he has more reason for wanting it than he imagines. But I did not exhaust the reasons why the average person will not knowingly do what is wrong.

Above and beyond punishment by himself and others, the average person intuitively knows that wrong action is both immoral and inexpedient. He intuitively knows that right action is both expedient and good. He wants to be right when he can. He wants to be right so uniformly that he cannot ordinarily take wrong action without first convincing himself that, in this instance, it is right. In other words, he wants to be right. It is a primal urge that he will gratify whenever he can.

From the foregoing statements, it follows that the average person not only wants to be right, but he is also convinced that he *is* right. He believes that what he does is fair and honest. When he isn't convinced, he changes his behavior simply to live at peace with himself.

It is true that under sufficient temptation, the average person may cross the line of what he ordinarily considers honest. But he somehow rationalizes his act—before, during and after its occurrence. He may have to struggle to do it particularly if someone challenges him. Sometimes that takes a lot of ingenuity, but he tries to come up with a plausible story. Often the fact that he protests too much gives him away. If you confront him in an indefensible position and destroy his carefully fabricated explanation, you inflict emotional wounds that may cause him to dislike you for a long time. The reason is that he is ashamed of his dishonesty; it is a reflection of the fact that he wants to look right, especially in the eyes of others.

That is another way of saying that it is dangerous to question openly any person's honesty. And it leads me to state that I have no intention of questioning anybody's. That is his job, not mine. But if he learns as much by questioning his as I have learned by questioning mine—an act, I think, too few people pursue—he'll certainly be glad he did.

Not only does the average person want to be right and to feel convinced that he is right, he also has an instinctive desire to see his inner convictions justified by the events of life. He wants to see right win out. He is somehow dissatisfied with a novel or movie in which right does not triumph.

At this point, I would add a word of caution that anyone who gets his knowledge of right and wrong from novels and movies has wide areas of misinformation.

Despite all these tendencies of the average person to be right, he often falls into error. If you closely observe practically anyone during a reasonable length of time, you will see clear-cut violations of honesty within the strict terms of this book; some of those terms have yet to be defined. However, they are not so strict but that a victim of such dishonesty would invariably agree with the terms, provided only that he is sufficiently aware of what occurred.

You will see examples of dishonesty that seemingly violate the perpetrator's own expressed standards of conduct. What those examples of inconsistency show is not that he lacks standards of conduct. He has them whether he realizes it or not. So far as he is aware of them, he is usually proud of his standards even when they are erroneous. Often he is quite frank in discussing them. He almost always lives by them, whatever they are.

That brings us to the statement that the average person is usually scrupulous about observing the generally recognized standards of conduct considered sound, and he is equally scrupulous about observing his additional personal standards, whatever they are. He would be ashamed to do otherwise, and his shame is enough to keep certain dishonest urges in check. But you have doubtless observed that there is a wide variation in the personal standards of conduct among different people. What one person does easily is outside the pale for another.

As stated, the average person will not pick your pocket. He might pick your mind. He will not bear false witness against you. He might cop off the glory for one of your accomplishments. It all depends on what his standards permit.

There is another kind of inconsistency that afflicts the average person. He has one set of standards for his friends, another and lower one for strangers, perhaps a still lower one for "soulless" corporations, and his lowest is reserved for the people he dislikes, especially his enemies. Most people think that attitude is natural. For anybody who considers it good practice, I should like to suggest that he keep his mind open on the subject.

Since I have shown why I feel optimistic about the average person's ability to live up to his standards of behavior whatever they are, in the next chapter, I shall paint the other side of the picture.

Chapter 5

Many Individuals Are Confused

ONCE I parked my car in a nearby city while I delivered a lecture. When I returned to the car, it bore a ticket for illegal parking. "Stop in at City Hall," the ticket warned, "and pay your fine." I did.

A week later I went to the same city and appeared before the same audience. During my talk, I casually mentioned the parking ticket. A member of the audience spoke up. "Why didn't you bring the ticket with you tonight?" he asked. "I could have saved you some money."

Other members of the group were not to be outdone. Ability to fix a traffic ticket, it seemed, was not unusual. I asked the group, "How many of you could have fixed that ticket for me?" As far as I could see, every hand went up. To make sure that my eyes were not deceiving me, I put the question in reverse. "Is there anyone in this room who could not have fixed that ticket?" Not a hand went up.

That was an audience of intelligent and well-educated men. Many were executives, attending a meeting sponsored by a prominent religious organization. Each one, I feel sure, would have instantly resented any aspersion on his personal integrity.

According to the definition used in this book, those men were not honest.

I realize that there are many persons who see nothing wrong in using political pull to avoid a fine. Many are proud of their ability to do it and consider it smart. They would be genuinely astonished to hear anyone suggest that they are the sort of people who are putting the skids under our national freedom.

Maybe you think I am magnifying a trivial point. But, quite definitely, the point is not trivial. It shows a flaw in our national character; one that should be corrected.

If occasionally a person has a traffic ticket fixed, he should forsake that convenience in the future. In doing so, that particular practice will be replaced with a concept far more valuable than money.

While you are reading what is to come, it is helpful to remember that the average person who does what is wrong is more a victim of error than a miscreant. What he needs, therefore, is help, not censure. Keeping that fact in mind, helps a person to avoid some emotional shocks.

These theories and principles have been more than twenty years in development. During that time, I discovered and corrected many habitual errors in my own thinking. How many, I could not say; I am still finding them.

One reason is that, in my student days, I had teachers who quite unintentionally taught me concepts that were not true, resulting in conclusions that were false. Similarly the average person has numerous unsuspected false notions that he reasons from daily. They continue to deliver wrong conclusions until they are corrected. It necessarily follows that those uncritically accepted false notions distort thinking in considering the topics to which they relate. I am going to write frankly about that problem, and in developing my subject, I shall talk about ethics.

Several friends and advisers recommended that I should not write about ethics because it is a dull, academic subject and people are not interested. Nonetheless it is included because ignoring ethics is what is keeping society locked in many kinds of trouble.

If ignoring the study of ethics meant only that people were turning their backs on a dull subject, ethics could safely be overlooked, but that is not the case. Ignoring ethics leads to a sort of ignorance that threatens our whole way of life.

Personally, I am an ethics zealot, because I am certain that virtually all our public and private problems are basically ethical in nature.

What does the word "ethics" really mean?

The dictionary defines ethics as the discipline that treats of morals and right behavior. I should like to repeat a few principles that elaborate on that definition. They are the same principles earlier cited that are supported in the next several pages.

Here are those principles:

Right cannot be wrong. Wrong cannot be right. Right action cannot lead to wrong results. Wrong action cannot lead to right results. Wrong action has to lead to wrong results. Right action has to lead to right results. Therefore, everybody owes it to himself to think, say and do what is right and to refuse to think, say or do what is wrong.

The reason so many people dispute those principles is that they think they have seen exceptions to them. Personally I never have, although I have seen what looked like exceptions. Analysis of many hundreds of those seeming exceptions revealed that there were none. What I did learn as a result of those analyses was astonishing.

One thing I learned is that refusal to accept those statements leads to personal confusion. The following is a small example:

Recently I submitted an article on human relations to a national magazine. When it came back with several passages crossed out, I discussed them with the editor. He commented that the indicated passages were not about human relations but about ethics, and they were off the subject.

That thinking is commonly shared. One of the reasons for difficult human relations is the belief that ethics has nothing to do with the subject. In reality, ethics is a prime consideration, because the basic point is usually a moral one. Yet if you go into almost any institution of learning, you discover that human relations, in certain phases, is taught in a manner that contradicts sound, commonly accepted ethical points. Those contradictions are seldom challenged.

Consider salesmanship, for example.

Who can deny that millions of salespeople are trained to advance the strong points in a presentation while concealing the weak ones? There are people who believe that such practice is the essence of salesmanship.

I remember being taught to take the weakest point in an article of merchandise and convert it into the strongest. When the price is too high, say, "It pays to spend a little more and get the best." When cheap construction has been used, say, "Our engineers have devised a way of getting more strength with less material." There are other tricks, and many salespeople utilize them when necessary to land an order. Indeed, such tactics are considered smart.

Consider debating.

My own training included the following rather astonishing statement: A good debater is one who can get on either side of a question and win. Those people say that such is the essence of debating. I have watched debaters advance arguments they knew were specious and accept applause from an audience who knew that sound ethics had been discarded. I submit that no debate can be honest unless each participant is wholly sincere; yet the sincere approach is often considered not practical. Does the average person prefer sophistry?

Consider advertising.

A manufacturer of hosiery took out some threads from

his product, leaving the original thickness only in the heel and toe. Then he advertised that the heel and toe were reinforced. To his friends, he frankly admitted that his advertising was a lie, but it did increase sales to unsuspecting consumers.

That sort of deception is not only taught in schools of advertising, but I have known them to use the same sort of dishonesty in seeking enrollments.

Consider public relations.

Many experts assert that the purpose of public relations is to mold public opinion to be favorable to a company, a product or an individual. The right approach is to analyze whether the company, product or individual is sound; then to take stock of weaknesses and errors; correct them; and finally see to it that the public gets an accurate impression of the facts. Certainly it is right to correct errors in the public mind, but is that the way public relations are handled? I have often seen them handled, seldom in that way.

The usual procedure is more like the approach employed by a supervisor of schools quoted in a newspaper column, "Sing the strengths of the school and its teachers always."

It is generally agreed that our schools, colleges and universities should not present teachings that contradict the known principles of ethics. But how can a person invariably distinguish between right and wrong? My analyses indicate that distinctions between right and wrong are ordinarily clear-cut, but I have analyzed many in which the confused person was victimized by his own wrong thoughts.

This is a typical example.

Recently I talked with a man whose intelligence I respect. In his special field, he knows how to solve problems and get things done. He told me of a speaker he had heard whose topic had been "Preserve the American Way of Life."

My informant said, "That speaker was good. He spoke of

how much graft and corruption infest our government. He cited examples. He named names and described the sort of bait and deals that help swing an election."

As my informant described the ovation accorded that speaker, I wondered how many other listeners, when it seemed to their advantage, had resorted to the dishonesty they condemned. I knew my informant was not blameless.

Several months earlier he had told me how he had obtained a building permit. "If you walk into City Hall with your hat in hand, you'll see a politician reading a newspaper behind his desk. He'll let you stand and wait for a while before he hears your request. Then, if he has any reason to deny your request, he'll do it. But someone tipped me off to the right procedure. You carry a book under your arm and put a bill in it for a bookmark. You let the end of the money stick out where the politician can see it. "Even if there are several people ahead of you, the politician will beckon, get you aside, and find out what you want. You tell him. While you are telling him, you put the book where you can't see it, but he can. Pretty soon he gives you what you want, you take your book and leave. When you get outside, you find the money is gone."

My informant had chuckled in obvious delight. "I tried it, and it worked!"

It is a curious anomaly that this man could have been so inconsistent in his thinking. I said that I respected his intelligence, but that respect is confined to the areas in which his intelligence is valid. In other areas, I fear his stupidity.

Especially I fear the results of the same sort of stupidity on the part of millions of people, all bent on using shortcuts in getting their way, pursuing their special interests while condemning others who employ the same shortcuts while pursuing theirs.

For people in the mass, there is a sharp difference

between what is practiced and what is preached. The unfortunate result is that what is practiced is embodied in our system of doing business and our system of government.

Some people resist the dishonest system as did the head of a construction firm. He went into that same City Hall. In a loud voice, he told every politician who blocked him, "If you try to deny that permit, you are violating the law. I'm entitled to it, and it's your duty to provide it. If you do not, what am I to think except that you want a payoff from my company? Do you want to make an issue of it?"

He got what he needed and saved thousands of payoff dollars that previously had been routine.

I have reported that story partly to show that the person who insists on what is right and refuses to accept what is wrong can use that approach to advance his interests. As a matter of fact, it is the right thing to do. Another example of this seemingly honest head of a construction firm shows his unsuspected departure from right.

Some years ago he wanted to make a long train trip. Because all the accommodations were sold out, he sneaked into a sleeping car on the train he wanted to take, locked himself in a drawing room and went to bed as fast as he could. When the holder of the correct ticket arrived, he couldn't get in. By the time the conductor was summoned, the train was under way. When the conductor knocked, the occupant was indignant, threatened to report the conductor and have his company boycott that railroad in the future. The conductor was only too glad to settle the matter by taking advantage of a drawing room left vacant by a patron who had missed the train.

The proud construction man continued, "Next morning there was a different conductor. When he saw me, he was mad as a hornet, but I was all apologies. I told him I had been so tired and in such a hurry that my judgment must have deserted me. Then I gave him a generous tip, and when he left, we were like old friends."

Many conflicting ideas went through my mind during the foregoing recital, and there were several things I wanted to say. I decided to try one. "Could it be that your generous tip was a bribe?" I asked.

"Oh, no. It would've been a bribe if I'd given it to the conductor in advance. I wouldn't do that. I don't condone bribery!"

What shortsightedness could so distort the thinking of an obviously intelligent man? We are coming to that.

Consider next the case of a prominent law firm headed by a congressman. A client who had overparked brought in a parking ticket with the request that it be handled. In a routine way, the congressman turned the ticket over to an assistant. As soon as the client was gone, an onlooker who disliked such practices voiced his objections and asked if anything could be done to stop it. "The practice is wrong," said the congressman, "and should be stopped. I'll join and support any movement to that effect, but under present conditions, there is nothing I can do about it. Every law firm in the city fixes traffic tickets for its clients. Most know it is wrong. But every lawyer knows that if he refused to do it, he would simply hand the business to his competitors."

I could go on with a long series of such cases, but there is no need. The average person knows about them. However, not everybody realizes that society is caught in a vicious mental trap that needs to be exposed.

Chapter 6

Masses of People Are Dishonest

THE PURPOSE of this chapter is to show that masses of people, individually and collectively, are dishonest. We shall start with a discussion of stealing. If anyone should think stealing an inconsequential form of dishonesty that few people practice, he will stop thinking it before finishing this chapter.

One reason we are going to talk about stealing is that it represents dishonesty in one of its more spectacular forms. Another is that the person who commits a direct act of stealing can hardly be thought unconscious of that dishonesty. But the main reason is that the person who steals thereby demonstrates a willingness to steal. If he will steal, it is reasonable to assume that he will engage in other forms of dishonesty with a less recognized flavor of wrong than stealing—of which there are many.

Here are a few basic facts:

There are laws against robbing your neighbor's house. Thus laws formalize a prohibition against an act that everybody knows is wrong, and no matter what the moral aspect, those laws were established for the public's protection. If people everywhere were honest, such laws would not be necessary.

In the moral sense, the thing that is wrong about robbing your neighbor's house is not that it is against the law. The law merely recognizes a principle and tries to force people to live by that principle. The same principle is given other forms of legal recognition. It is illegal to rob anybody's house. It is illegal to rob a pedestrian, a train, a corporation, a government, or any other individual or group. That is, it is illegal to rob by the direct physical act of stealing any of a person's tangible possessions.

What is wrong about stealing? Discard the legal aspects, and think only of moral considerations.

By stealing, you get something to which you are not entitled. At the expense of somebody else, you get something you have not earned nor paid for in toil or wealth. You deprive someone of a possession that is rightfully his and compel him to make a sacrifice against his will. To do any of those things is morally wrong as is recognized by numerous laws.

The laws specifically define and forbid stealing, but there are also many apparently unrelated laws that, in a sense, are prohibitions against stealing. They prohibit subtracting from the rights of others, against taking something of tangible or intangible value to which a person is not entitled and that he can get only by detriment to someone else.

It is easy to see the connection to stealing with laws against bribery or graft. But reflect on laws against barking dogs that prevent people from stealing their neighbors' sleep and peace of mind; laws against parking that prevent a motorist from stealing space more urgently needed for another purpose; laws favoring public health that prevent one person's negligence from stealing, perhaps, the health of an entire city. Analysis of many laws shows that the principle that stealing is wrong is somehow involved.

Many forms of stealing are illegal, but there are others that are not. Yet the principle against stealing extends beyond those laws. By definition, a principle is a universal truth. Therefore, the principle applies equally to the other ways of stealing in which no infraction of man-made law is involved. People instinctively know it.

They also know that there are people who have made themselves rich by taking advantage of opportunities to steal within the law.

There are people who will steal whether it is legal or not. The more intelligent they are and the more they know about the laws and their legal loopholes, the more dangerous those . people will be.

Then there are people who will not steal because it is wrong. No laws are needed to hold those people in check; they can be trusted with the keys to your car and house. But society has not yet developed means for protecting itself against the people who will steal when stealing is legal. What is needed is a way of raising those people to the moral level of those who will not steal because it is wrong. That would give us a moral utopia so far as stealing is concerned.

Before me is a news clipping quoting a group of bankers praising the honesty of the average citizen. Those bankers call him honest because he seldom fails to repay a bank loan. If the clipping represents their real view, they misunderstand what fundamental honesty implies. I presume their remarks come under the head of public relations.

When an average person borrows from a bank, unless he is already known to the loan officer, he is investigated. Unless he is proved financially responsible, he doesn't get the loan. Therefore, the bankers should praise their ability to select borrowers who can and will repay, for that is what the repayment statistics really mean.

How much confidence a bank has in the average person is partly shown by the check protectors it uses, the surety bonds it requires on its employees, the watchmen and guards it employs, the locks on its doors and vaults, the burglar alarms and theft insurance that protect its assets, and the chains on the pens in its lobbies. Those things do not reflect on the bankers. They reflect on the average person.

Under the usual safeguards our society has set up, it is perhaps true that few persons would commit an outright theft. But the lock industry is founded on the fact that there are enough thieves to make people's possessions unsafe unless they are protected. In a really honest society there would be no lock industry, no credit agencies, no detectives, fewer laws, fewer jails and fewer policemen.

Subway exit turnstiles are so constructed as to prevent dishonest patrons from entering through them to evade payment of fare. Slot-machine turnstiles are made with a magnifying glass window so that a slug is more easily detected. The cashier is enclosed in a grilled compartment to prevent patrons from reaching in and stealing coins.

When a passenger boards a railroad train, he is supposed to have a ticket purchased from a ticket agent. He gets it through a small hole in a wall protected by a metal grille so that nobody can reach into the hole to grab a handful of money. After boarding the train, the conductor is supposed to see that he really hands in the ticket instead of saving it to use on the next trip.

Maybe the average person is honest, but riding on a local train, I have often seen passengers taking advantage of opportunities to save their tickets. I have seen holders of commutation tickets slyly picking up the bit of cardboard punched out by the conductor to fill the hole so the same square can be punched again.

Over the years, no less than thirty people have suggested that tricky procedure to me. It was done with an air of letting me in on a profitable secret. None of them would have picked my pocket, robbed my house or cheated me in an ordinary business deal. But all of them thought it proper to cheat the railroad company. "After all," said one, "they have lots of money."

I know a restaurant where you figure your own bill. On the way out, the diner tells the cashier what he owes and pays it. That restaurant made a reputation out of trusting its patrons. I ate there once and discovered how far that trust goes. When I stated the amount of my bill to the cashier, he called out the figure in a voice that could have filled a large auditorium. Why? My guess is that he was instructed to give the patrons a chance to check up on each other's honesty— and also to shame a diner if he needed it.

If people must be shamed into honesty even in a minor financial transaction, they are not honest. Clearly our society is not geared to an assumption that the average person is honest. It is geared to an assumption that he is not.

Even if a person accepts the belief that the average person will almost always do the right thing, he takes precautions. He habitually counts his change, keeps an eye on his possessions, takes out burglary insurance and keeps his valuables in a safe deposit box. There are prudent motorists who seldom drive anywhere without locking themselves in their cars. I am one of them. The locked doors are to prevent someone from forcing his way into my car to steal it, my money and my life while I am waiting at a traffic light. That sort of thing is being done.

Let us next consider how many people will commit the act of stealing when the usual safeguards are down.

Once I stopped at a little restaurant in a rural community. Just before I arrived, a truck loaded with chickens had upset several hundred feet down the road. The damaged crates were strewn across an open field, and chickens roamed all over the countryside.

Soon a line of cars collected. Motorists got out to help the driver capture chickens. They had a field day. With few exceptions, those motorists put the chickens they caught into their own cars. The operator of a nearby gasoline station herded several into his washroom. The restaurant owner collected some in his cellar. The truck driver regained less than half his original load.

A druggist put an umbrella into one of his telephone booths for the explicit purpose of testing his customers' honesty. Twenty times during the first day, he caught a customer in the act of leaving with that umbrella. To avoid embarrassment that might have wrecked his business, the druggist had to discontinue his experiment.

Consider two more cases:

A student lost his trunk. One year later it was discovered in a college dormitory where it had been left when he transferred to another school. Only two unattractive items were in it. Shortly afterward, he called at his old dormitory, visiting among his former friends. He said nothing about the trunk, but he saw his alarm clock, typewriter, tennis racket, several books and various items of his clothing in possession of his former fellow students.

An air force officer shot down over enemy territory, unexpectedly returned sometime later to discover that all his possessions had been redistributed. Even his wallet, officially turned in for safekeeping, was missing several hundred dollars. He is a bit cynical about what his buddies will do when their honesty is put under the strain of tempting opportunity.

The examples just given are not questionable cases. Each involved stealing. They involved dishonesty that is punishable under law when it is proved. They involved a number of culprits. They show that even the dishonesty of stealing can and does occur on what amounts to a mass basis, and also what the average person may do when he sees the chance to get away with it. However, there are many kinds of widespread dishonesty that are harder to detect.

Consider the person who pockets money he finds without seeking its owner, the person who mails personal letters at his employer's expense, who accepts an excessive amount of change when making a purchase, or who drives away from a car he has damaged while parking. Consider the tradesman who overcharges, the waiter who gives short change, the repairman who bills you for work not done, the professional who takes advantage of people's ignorance to sell unneeded services, or the one who makes his services seem complicated to justify an exorbitant fee. All those practices are dishonest.

There are also kinds of dishonesty that the average person does not consider dishonest. When he thinks they will advance his cause, he has no hesitation about using them.

Consider the person who pushes ahead in a line of patrons at a store or restaurant, the automobile driver who parks double or squeezes ahead at a traffic light, the person who demands extra service and chisels on the price, the person who makes a promise he cannot keep, and the person who plays all the angles and works both ends against the middle under an assumption that he is using his head. It would be easy to fill a book with common examples of that sort of dishonesty.

Probably nobody could read very far without recognizing various kinds of dishonesty that he has occasionally practiced himself. I can't, and I am not proud of that. When we do such things, it is easy to delude ourselves that one individual is hardly important. But it isn't a case of one individual. Such things are done by millions of people every day. The resulting chaos in our mass character is frightening.

It is almost correct to say that the only reasonably honest person is the one who will admit that he has been repeatedly dishonest, with himself and others, and has done it so habitually that he has long since ceased to notice it even in his own mind.

There are people who will defend and justify their dishonesty because it is minor and infrequent. But *the person who is ninety-eight percent honest is still two percent dishonest, and that is enough to throw his whole life off the track.* Nobody is dishonest all the time, not even the most hardened criminal.

Perhaps this discussion would lead a reader to suppose that I have gone about looking for examples of dishonesty. Occasionally I have. "Of course," he may say, "anyone who looks for dishonesty will find it." That is true. But it is also true that dishonesty cannot be found where it does not exist. The truth is that it can be found almost anywhere.

Consider some additional cases.

The manufacturer who produces dishonest or dangerous merchandise. The salesman who tricks a prospective customer's mind. The union that makes jobs where no jobs exist. The person who concocts an explanation of a failure that was due to his personal negligence, who takes or accepts credit for somebody else's achievement, who undermines his competitors or who damages the interests of persons he considers opponents or enemies. The employer who improperly takes advantage of extra work or special ability or unfairly restricts an employee's earnings, who denies opportunities to a promising subordinate for fear of his competition. The yes man who says only what he thinks his superiors want to hear. The worker who neglects his responsibilities, creates a false impression of knowledge and ability, gets by on inferior work, demands more than he is worth or otherwise fails to live up to the obligations implied in any working relationship.

Maybe you don't think such things occur very often, but I could write a book about any of the foregoing examples just by telling what I have seen. In fact, I'll expand one of them through another couple of paragraphs.

Workers often complain over unfairness from management, but what workers occasionally do to their employers is equally unfair. Consider the worker who instead of quitting gets himself fired after he has planned a vacation or accepted a position with another employer so that he can collect severance or vacation pay or fill in a few weeks' gap with unemployment payments.

Workers have developed an appalling number of devices for taking advantage of their employers. In almost every business organization, it is customary for workers to start late and quit early. When employers recognize that human tendency by giving a few minutes' leeway, the leeway is immediately added to the loss already suffered. When a rest period is provided during the day, the result is only that there is a new opportunity for early quitting and late starting. The condition is so general that the average employer will sputter when he hears the subject mentioned or perhaps shrug his shoulders in resignation.

Consider also the innumerable cases of individuals who will betray a public trust:

The medical intern or policeman who rob drunken or unconscious accident victims on the way to the hospital, the politicians who settle a brush with the law, contractors who "buy" municipal jobs, and politicians who "sell" them.

The office seeker who makes unreasonable campaign promises or who makes reasonable promises he does not keep. The voter who disregards public good and casts his ballot in return for dishonest advantage, and the politician or demagogue who tempts him to do it. The pressure groups formed to establish false programs, and the legislators who cringe before their organized selfishness. The masses of voters who raid our public treasury, and the legislators who dare not raise objections for fear of losing out in the next election.

By any reasonable definition, those people are all dishonest. But by no means have I exhausted the possible list. I have hardly scratched the surface of the dishonesty of our public servants, coroners, judges and magistrates, tax collectors, legislators and government administrators. I have discussed briefly the graft of petty politicians but have not shown how that graft is magnified on a national scale. I have not discussed what is dishonest about the management of corporations and unions, although every reader knows that those topics are both important. They have been omitted because including them would delay this book and make it too large for the average person to read.

There is only one formula that can rescue society from its mass dishonesty. Everybody should *think, say and do what is right and refuse to think, say and do what is wrong.*

Part II

Distinguishing Right From Wrong

Chapter 7

How To Determine What Is Right

THE UNDERLYING thesis of this book is that *dishonesty is wrong; dishonesty is widespread; dishonesty produces wrong action and frustrates right action; dishonesty destroys the effectiveness of human intellect, blinding people to the causes of individual and collective ills; dishonesty is the basic threat to society's welfare and way of life and that it is time something was done to correct it.* It is an obvious thesis, but the average person has not been moved by it or correction would have been made long ago. Instead, people have the delusion that problems and troubles are caused by other factors.

To explain that delusion, let us review the methods by which a person learns to distinguish between right and wrong. Let us consider those methods as they are and as they should be in a society sufficiently versed in scientific method to have developed the atom bomb.

So far as we know, a child comes into this world without knowledge. At first, he lives completely under the management of his parents. A duty of his parents is to transfer that management, by gradual steps, to the child himself. The process begins in the first years of life and normally continues through his teens. During the process, specialized help is obtained from outside training agencies, notably schools. It is presumed to be a simple duty for parents to provide knowledge of self-management techniques that enable the child to develop normally and become a productive member of society.

As a part of that process, whether by accident or design, the child acquires standards of moral behavior. Parental supervision includes seeing that proper standards are provided, that improper standards are kept from developing, and seeing that outside influences leading to error are counteracted. The child who is taught a sound moral code enjoys a favored existence and avoids much trouble.

When parents fail to teach proper standards, they find themselves confronted with what is known as a problem child. It has been argued that there are no problem children but only parents who have neglected a basic duty and are themselves problem parents. But that seems unfair to parents, because they tend to pass along a version of what they had been taught in the same general way. If that version is sufficiently flawed, we have both problem parents and problem children. The root cause then becomes problem ancestors.

Broadly speaking, no child or teen is responsible for his wrong behavior. Parental and ancestral delinquency should divide the responsibility. The child becomes responsible only as he learns standards of right behavior. If he must devise those standards for himself, it seems unreasonable to expect him to do it while still a child.

The child should be taught standards of behavior that keep him out of trouble. To achieve that, those standards must be sufficiently comprehensive that they also prevent his causing trouble for others. Parents sometimes neglect to instill the familiar standards, but, more serious, they lack knowledge of standards that are sufficiently comprehensive to serve. That is not the fault of the parents. They simply pass along portions of an incomplete inheritance.

It is time to break up that sort of thing. It is time to insist that suitable standards of behavior be found and put into general circulation.

Some experts claim that the average person never grows up. That is, he never matures morally, emotionally and intellectually. It is argued that people are not supposed to mature intellectually, and with that I agree. To mature, according to my dictionary, means to attain full growth. In that sense I hope to mature intellectually for many more decades.

What those experts mean is that the average person stops growing intellectually before he stops growing physically. When that happens, it is certain that he also stops growing morally and emotionally. Unless he has already reached moral and emotional maturity, cessation of intellectual growth is calamitous.

While nature takes care of a person's physical growth, moral and emotional development is largely delegated to him. The continued use of intellect is essential, because the person who stops growing intellectually before he is morally and emotionally mature becomes a moral and emotional cripple who then destroys much of the intellectual growth he had already attained.

In this book, I am not concerned with physical growth, but I am concerned with moral growth. To reach moral maturity demands the knowledge of comprehensive and reliable standards of behavior that automatically protect the individual against moral error in every area of his life.

Insofar as I have been able to develop such standards, they are embodied in this book. It is my conviction that all those standards are undebatable and inarguable and that their general adoption would transform society's way of life.

I know how much work it took to produce those standards, and I had the advantage of what I consider sound moral training to get me started. *The principle of absolute right is based on a natural law of behavior that I discovered while working out my own moral code.* The lack of widespread knowledge of that law is why there is individual and collective dishonesty on a mass scale. That is also why I am not inclined to blame anybody.

The child who is unknowingly guilty of an antisocial act would not be blamed for it by an understanding parent. The adult who is unknowingly guilty of an antisocial act would not be blamed for it by an understanding contemporary. But when either one is knowingly guilty of outright dishonesty, he should be held accountable.

First, consider how the average person actually gets his standards of behavior in contrast with the way he should get them.

To a small child, right is perhaps what Mother wants him to do: go to bed at bedtime, eat his food, brush his teeth, and such things as those. Wrong is what Mother doesn't want him to do: engage in forbidden mischief, take dangerous risks, lie to her, and so on. Unless Mother overtaxes her wisdom, much is likely to be satisfactory about the standards of right and wrong thus established. In any event a small child quickly learns that right is what you are supposed to do and wrong is what you are not supposed to do. He absorbs an inclination to be right, in that sense, that lasts throughout life. In proportion to the extent he flouts it, he is made miserable.

At first, the penalty for wrong action is trouble with Mother, and similarly the reward for right action is Mother's approval. Gradually the child learns that failure to be right leads to trouble with nature, and that lesson is the beginning of wisdom for him.

He learns that distinctions between right and wrong are not arbitrary expressions of maternal authority based on the fact that she is big enough to enforce her authority. At least, that is what he learns if Mother is conscientious and mature. If she selfishly allows her emotions to decide what is right, the child never learns that **natural distinctions of right and** *wrong are self-enforcing: attempted violations of gravity bring bumps, bruises and broken bones. He needs to learn that dishonesty naturally brings impairment to his intellect.* There is one basic reason why Mother must interpret the distinctions between right and wrong for her child. She saves herself trouble by insisting on good behavior, and she also saves the child from possible risk of a fatal lesson. The fatal lesson may come later in adult life, because the penalties of wrong action are inexorable, and ignorance is no excuse. Mother's job is to protect the child against that ignorance until he has learned to protect himself.

If there are brothers and sisters, property rights are likely to be understood early. Human nature being what it is, a child learns that he can expect consideration for what is his only if he gives consideration for what belongs to others. When he gets into trouble, it is oftener because he failed to respect other persons' rights than because he failed to remember his own. It is helpful if he has brothers and sisters to remind him. Few average adults have failed to learn the principle of property rights as children, although later they may fail to respect that knowledge.

There is a prevalent theory that most emotional trouble in adults springs out of the frustrations of childhood. Approached carefully, frustration can be used to encourage a child's development. The child who is shielded from frustration may fail to learn how to deal with it.

A person can argue the pros and cons of early frustration, but he cannot argue the pros and cons of teaching a child to be honest. The child who never learns to be honest is in for trouble that inevitably he will share with those around him. *The child who learns to be honest deals with his early frustrations by extracting their value.*

Medical research papers are dotted with case histories of

people who got into trouble because they were dishonest in their private thoughts. Indeed, certain kinds of dishonesty have been classified, given high-sounding names, and called emotional diseases. If we call them what they are, we can eliminate them, and the best time to start is in childhood.

The basis of intellectual dishonesty is the lie. Lying requires creative ingenuity. The child who lies, and every imaginative child has done it many times, knows that he is lying at the time. Childhood affords ample opportunity for a parent to expose more than one lie to the child and to let him know that the parent knows he has lied. It affords the opportunity to discuss temptations to lie and to see that lying evokes proper attention.

The child who suffers frustration may blight his development, which I question, but the child who lies impairs his intellect. If people would cut in half the time spent on preventing frustration and use the time saved to frustrate the habit of lying, they wouldn't need so much mental health attention in later years.

There is a reason why I have singled out lying for the foregoing rather drastic attention. It is that children generally are told not to lie by their parents, but simultaneously through force of example, they are taught to lie by the same parents.

One of the reasons why it is less usual for children to steal than lie is because parents usually hide from their children that example of dishonesty. Children lie despite their parents' expressed objections because most parents lie in the presence of their children often enough to contradict their own teachings. They are so accustomed to lying that they do it quite automatically. What they accomplish is to train their children to believe that a lie is wrong only when a person gets caught. As a result, children learn to increase their negative ingenuity to avoid getting caught.

While it is thought that the average child gets his moral training by direct instruction, that is only partly true. Most of his moral training he gets by force of example.

Example consists in what the child sees other people do. He gets examples from his peers, many of which should be counteracted, and he also gets examples from his elders. Since his elders are naturally imposing and more experienced, the child usually accepts uncritically what he observes. When he sees dishonesties that seem to work, he tends to adopt those practices. It puts the child in an anomalous position to find himself being punished for copying the behavior of his elders. No lecture on honesty is likely to be heeded when it flies in the face of example.

Example constitutes the most universal training medium for behavior, and it consists largely of what most people do. No thoughtful person would disagree that a person cannot learn what is right by observing what most people do. In addition, such observation often provides only half the lesson. When a child observes one of his elders in the performance of a wrong act, usually he sees only the act. Whenever possible, the penalty is concealed. Parents usually take pains to see that trouble resulting from their wrong action occurs in the child's absence. Most often, the parents do not realize there is even any connection between the wrong act and the resulting trouble.

If parents, by force of example, teach wrong action to their children, it is only fair to show the child every resulting penalty. Parents who live up to that obligation become cautious about getting into trouble, which is to say that they learn to do what is right and avoid doing what is wrong.

What people generally do constitutes a definition of custom. *It is obvious that custom is a device by which dishonesty has been transmitted from one generation to the next, passed along in the form of behavior and conversation.* It is also passed along in the form of specific training which generally carries a flavor of improvement over custom. The improvement comes out of the fact that home, school and religious training often disapproves of certain elements of custom. So the child learns that custom affords no infallible standards for what is right. He may learn that custom modified by what is approved by the people he respects affords a better standard.

That is still not a reliable guide as it allows wide gaps in standards of behavior. Often it allows a person to be taught wrong behavior, because it leaves the subject of approval open to individual interpretation by fallible adults. Society needs fixed standards. Standards so elemental that when understood can be interpreted as easily by a child as by an adult.

There are certain arbitrary standards that are acceptable. In this category are the rules of a game arrived at by common consent or a rule book. So long as the rules apply equally to every participant, they are fair. So long as they make the game interesting, they serve their purpose. In the final analysis, whether they are right or wrong is not a moral question.

When a child learns the rules of a game, he also learns to respect rules in various other forms by implication. He learns to respect the rules of a school, later the rules of a business organization, and similarly to respect local and national laws.

There are two things wrong with that sort of moral training. First, as children are learning to respect rules and laws, they are also observing apparently successful infraction of those rules and laws by the adults to whom they look for guidance. Second, it is difficult to allow for the fact that often the rules and laws themselves are partly or wholly wrong.

Wrongness in a rule or law may occasionally compel a person to do what is forbidden to stay out of trouble. For example, I once avoided an automobile accident by disregarding a red traffic signal. However, it is true that few laws and rules tend to prevent right action. It is more likely that unfair laws and rules exact a penalty. For example, a person may be forced to pay an unfair income tax. There is nothing he can rightly do to protect his interests until fairness is injected into the law. Those two examples show that *rules and laws are only an expression of fallible minds attempting to convert moral right into practical forms.*

By attempting to obey parental instructions, the child learns early that man-made laws and rules are often unjust. He would be less confused if more parents admitted their fallibility in establishing rules. He would learn more quickly that man-made laws and rules are an effort to interpret natural rules and laws. He would then be better able to understand that occasionally he must satisfy an unreasonable teacher and later an unreasonable boss if he understood that they also are prone to error. Above all, he would learn that *natural rules and laws are basic, and that he should look beneath the man-made version for the real thing.*

Natural law rather quickly impinges on childish consciousness. Such things as burned fingers, bumps, barked shins and broken toys bring his first knowledge of physics. Success and failure in dealing with people bring his first knowledge of human relations. With a minimum of parental guidance, he learns that what is right gets good results, while what is wrong gets bad results. Under that sort of guidance, the child quickly learns that trouble is caused and does not just happen.

Dishonesty is not an inherent trait. The child learns other things more easily than he learns dishonesty. That is obvious from the fact that his first efforts at dishonesty are naively crude, and only with practice does he become adept. Certainly his creative ability deserves higher use, for dishonesty is a prostitution of that creative ability to destructive use.

He can easily be shown that pretending a hot stove is cold does not prevent his getting burned when he touches it. From that simple beginning, the seeds of basic honesty begin to germinate. *Dishonesty is always a pretense that things are different from what they are, and that is exactly why dishonesty confuses the person who uses it as a tool of thought.* He tends to believe his own pretenses.

Often it is said that small children show greater ability to distinguish right from wrong than adults. Perhaps that is because the small child has not had time to develop his dishonesty. It should be emphasized that *the process of developing dishonesty consists of just two things: ability to fool other people and ability to fool oneself.* When a person tries to fool the law of gravity, he gets hurt, and the same is true in relation to any other natural law.

It is established that one way to be right is to behave in strict accord with natural law. It might be that a person does not know all the natural laws, but he gets into trouble mostly by flouting the laws that are known.

Natural law says that one plus one equals two. Any other answer is wrong. Any person who tries to establish another answer is trying to establish what is wrong. Clearly the act of trying to establish what is wrong constitutes wrong behavior. The person who does it is attempting to misrepresent a fact. If this book convinces people of the wisdom of refusing to misrepresent facts, society would achieve greater intellectual growth than could be imagined.

From the simple expedient of direct honesty, let us move to an entirely different approach. There are many ways to determine what is right that seemingly have little to do with honesty as such.

In a national political sense, for example, what is right is assumed to be what puts one's party into office and keeps it there. But if there were any similarity between the outcome of an election and what is right, it would be because enough honest voters made their honesty effective.

America is a democracy. In a democracy, it is said that the majority rules, but that is only partly true. Those who do not vote could alter the outcome of almost any election, because many voters customarily do not go to the polls. Moreover, a disproportionate percentage of voters tend to have dishonest incentives, because the lure of selfish gain is stronger than the desire for good citizenship. Despite all that, the candidates and issues able to collect the most votes win elections. Enough unprincipled voters could turn an election into a victory that is both immoral and wrong, imposing their negative will on others.

Let us examine another example.

At least in theory, our country is run by laws. Laws are made by legislators who are elected. Many powerful groups are interested in those laws. They stand to gain or lose depending on how the legislation is handled, and they have various ways of making their wishes known. They could state the facts and lobby to see that right thinking prevails.

Instead many such groups raise large treasuries, send out propaganda, enlist public support, magnify every evidence that their cause is right while, at the same time, minimizing every evidence that their cause is wrong. If possible, they threaten withdrawal of political support at the next election. They may even resort to outright bribery and other forms of dishonesty. They constitute what is known as pressure groups, and everybody knows that pressure influences the outcome of many legislative deliberations. So the fact must be acknowledged that dishonest pressure often becomes a means for deciding what is right.

Even a schoolchild recognizes that dishonest voting and

dishonest efforts to influence legislation are morally wrong, but many adults do not.

Existence of a pressure group is almost prima facie evidence of one purpose: to substitute personal force for logic. It is a device for winning despite the facts, and its use tends to destroy all recourse to the facts. In this society, the person with right on his side does not need personal pressure. Any temptation to use personal pressure should be his signal to check up on his morality and his logic. *The pressure is in the impersonal facts of the situation; those facts speak for themselves.*

The foregoing information may be difficult for a well-meaning person to accept. There are numerous militant groups waging incessant campaigns in favor of what they believe is right. Their leaders might ask, "What about pressure in favor of right?"

That is a good question, and it has a good answer.

In practically any field of human relations, meeting pressure with pressure gives an advantage to the side with greater deviation from facts. That side will be more devious, and other things being equal, will exert more pressure. That is why our network of pressure groups is counterproductive and does not really resolve our pressing problems.

There are many different kinds of pressure groups, and each apparently considers its cause little short of holy. Starting in the political scene with the most ruthless dictator, you can work your way down to the family scene in which the small child takes a toy away from a baby.

What makes a pressure group dangerous is the element of unfair persuasion by which it seeks to capture a decision. Remove the pressure and you remove the danger—a statement exactly as logical as it sounds.

In a national political sense, pressure can be defined as the outward expression of organized control over others.

The way to eliminate pressure is not to counter it with pressure. It is to use logic and present solid facts. *The group working for public good by honest procedures is not a pressure group and does not need to be militant.* What I have described are two criteria by which people determine what is right. They let opposing groups collide and argue with the aid of political and economic force until one side develops enough pressure to collect enough votes to get a decision. The two sides may be Republicans and Democrats, management and labor, capitalists and socialists, religious or racial opponents, and any other combination of groups having what they consider to be opposing interests.

Pressure groups are always at least partly wrong. They are formed to gain or perpetuate special privilege or to prevent the same things from being done by others. Pressure thrives on specious arguments, concealment of truth, collection of fraudulent political support. It is almost always wrong to create, support or yield to pressure. The only reasonable purpose of pressure is to counteract pressure that is unfair as when a policeman arrests a holdup man. When no infraction of law is involved, counteracting pressure is accomplished by simple exposure of truth. "Ye shall know the truth, and the truth shall make you free," is a wise teaching.

Unfortunately the temptation to create pressure is greater than the desire to counteract it, and often the opposition may not speak up for fear of reprisals.

All those difficulties and more tend to surround every expression of organized pressure, and most people know it. In view of that, it takes a mighty strong case to justify personal pressure for any cause whatever. The lesson is that society should neither tolerate nor support any form of such pressure, and that lacking clear-cut evidence, the voters and legislators should ignore organized pressure in favor of decisions dictated by logic and solid facts. In that event, our public issues could be approached on a basis of logical and honest reasoning. Pressure afflicts more than the political scene. There is also the pressure of personal authority in any form. People know what it is like to yield to an arbitrary decision made by a negligent or insincere person in a superior position. An executive may take unfair advantage of subordinates, and an organized group representing a pocket of entrenched dishonesty may impose its will on others.

When people are subjected to unfair treatment, human nature is such that they are tempted to fight back. But fighting is only another effort to substitute force for logic. At best, it is an attempt to use might to enforce right, and I must admit, it is often done.

When a person's life is in danger, it is difficult to justify an assumption that he should sacrifice it rather than fight, on either an individual or national basis. Most people think that it pays to be ready to defeat an enemy who threatens your extermination. The rights and wrongs of killing an enemy who threatens your life do not come within the scope of this book, so until somebody comes up with a logical reason against it, I shall continue to support preparedness. But I do think that it is wrong to fight when better means of establishing right are available as almost invariably they are.

Nevertheless, because of countless examples that start in early childhood and continue throughout our lives, fighting seems to be one of the procedures for deciding what is right. But fighting, like any other kind of pressure, is usually a way of handing the victory to the strongest and most unscrupulous adversary.

Instead of fighting, intelligent right action would lead to a satisfactory outcome, and it is well to remember that whenever temptation to fight arises. Fundamentally fighting is wrong as will be demonstrated in a succeeding chapter. Therefore, when fighting begins, the person who was right no longer is right—not completely. The result? He misses his opportunity to profit by the fact that right is might, whether you are talking about an individual or a nation.

Chapter 8

Defining Honesty and Dishonesty

$\mathbf{F}$ROM THE foregoing discussion, it is evident that the average person does not have properly established procedures for distinguishing between right and wrong. A young person is confronted with so much contradictory instruction and evidence that he grows up confused. Too often without knowing it, he continues to grow more confused as he matures. It is generally recognized that comprehensive principles are needed to dispel that confusion, and the purpose of this chapter is to present information about those principles.

Essentially this is a chapter of definition. Therefore, it is fitting that we turn to the dictionary for guidance. Four words call for attention.

Honesty: adherence to the facts; freedom from deceit; fairness; straightforwardness.

Dishonesty: lack of truth or integrity; disposition to defraud or deceive.

Right: in accordance with truth, justice or law; conforming to facts or truth; not mistaken; real, proper, fair, honest; genuine; correct.

Wrong: deviating from facts; injurious; unfair; something immoral, unethical; that which is contrary to right, justice, goodness, equity or law; incorrect.

The dictionary also gives enlightening synonyms for *honesty:* sincerity, fairness, integrity, probity, uprightness, rectitude, with the following further definition: *Honesty* is that quality of a person that shows him fair and truthful in speech, implying a refusal to lie, cheat, steal, or deceive in any other way.

Uprightness is that quality in man that carries him along a straight path of *honesty* and duty.

Integrity emphasizes the wholeness of man's moral nature; he is sound, incorruptible, and particularly strict about fulfilling the trusts reposed in him by others.

Probity is virtue which has been put to the test and never found wanting; adherence to the highest principles and ideals; it can be said that probity is demonstrated in honesty beyond a person's mere care for the property of others; he regards their good name, their every concern with the same conscience as he would his own.

Those are all commonsense definitions.

In certain scientific circles, common sense has taken a drubbing in recent years. It is said that there are higher levels of intelligence than common sense, and that I do not doubt. But it may be observed that when scientists neglect common sense, they get into the same trouble as other people, indicating the need to live on a plane of common sense before deserting it to go higher.

Among other things, I am referring to William James's assertion that truth is not necessarily what is in accord with fact. Despite the insight of his philosophy of pragmatism, I am going to assert that by advancing the theory that right is what works, James laid the foundation for a lot of unrecognized dishonesty in people's minds.

It would be better to say that what works is what is right, and to make it clear, what is not right will not work without some kind of detriment. Further, when a person asks an honest question, he deserves an honest answer. And to all practical purposes of ordinary life, an honest answer is factually correct.

It is on that level of common sense that this chapter is written. It hardly seems necessary to say that dishonesty is wrong. If proof were needed, it could be found in the frequency with which dishonesty causes problems and trouble; but this book is written for persons who do not dispute the point. In addition, it is written to reveal the cause and effect of dishonest action when people attempt to violate a natural behavioral law: ***right action gets right results, whereas wrong action gets wrong results.***

As a young person, developing his moral code, I was confronted with a trick question: A seriously ill woman asks about her son who has had an accident. She doesn't know it, but the son is dead. Any sudden shock could cause her death, too. Should you kill her by telling the truth, or should you protect her life by lying?

That type of question has thrown a lot of young minds into confusion.

I am not going to say how it should be answered; only that the moral answer is both expedient and true. And I should add that never, except when asked that sort of hypothetical question, have I been confronted with so complicated a choice. Ordinarily life confronts the average person with situations that would require greater ingenuity to concoct a wrong answer than to choose the right one.

I have seen a lot of people get into trouble by lying. Never have I seen anyone get into trouble by telling an intelligently managed truth. The person whose situation seems to call for a lie has made a wrong turn somewhere earlier. He did or said a wrong thing he feels obligated to protect. He should backtrack to make a correction, not add a lie to his earlier blunder.

There is also the question of diplomacy. When presentation of an unpalatable truth is required, the job should be done without friction and emotional damage. That may take careful thought. ***Resorting to a lie only shows lack of ability in handling human relations.*** It does not show that lying in that particular circumstance is right.

Lying is dishonest; therefore, it is wrong to deceive. The usual tool of deceit is the lie. A lie is an incorrect, false or untrue statement. It is untrue because it is not in accord with fact—with reality. But not every untrue statement is necessarily deceitful. Fiction, poetry and parables are all means for presenting ideas in imaginative form, and if the ideas are true to life, no deceit is involved. Nor is deceit involved in a clearly fictional story told for interest or amusement.

It is wrong to deceive by creating a false impression, by use of misleading words, by twisting the meanings of words, by concealing one side of a controversial issue, by exaggeration or understatement, or by misrepresentation of any sort. There are other ways of deceiving, and some of them do not involve speech. ***It is wrong to create a false impression by implication or by deed, by obscuring vital truth, by failure to provide essential information, by hypocrisy, pretense, insincerity or sham.***

To create an unintentional false impression is as wrong as to do it on purpose. In either case, the result is deception. Therefore, it is wrong to permit a false impression to be created by negligence. It is also wrong to let a false impression go uncorrected. To sum up, it is wrong to cause or permit deception by creating or failing to correct a false impression. Those issues that have no consequence to the deceiver, to the person deceived or to an innocent victim of the deceit can be eliminated. As stated, hair-splitting is seldom essential to practical application of the principle of absolute right: ***always think, say and do what is right; refuse to think, say and do what is wrong.***

In accord with the foregoing definitions, here are examples of dishonesty: the yes man who conceals information his boss might resent, the teacher who switches to a lesson that will show her to advantage when her supervisor enters the classroom, the driver whose direction signal shows turns that are not made, the person who varies facts according to what he is trying to prove, the debater who uses humor or ridicule to confuse issues or opponents, the politician who misrepresents a public issue.

Negligence and irresponsibility might be described as unintentional dishonesty. There may be disagreement that unintentional dishonesty is precisely as wrong as intentional dishonesty, but analysis will demonstrate that it is. Provable negligence in an accident case is actionable in court. Disastrous negligence by an employee is accepted as cause for discharge. Those are man-made regulations; for another point of view, let us turn to nature. When a person strikes the pavement at the base of a tall building, does nature adjust the penalty in accordance with whether he fell or jumped or was pushed purposely or by accident? The answer explains why negligence and irresponsibility are wrong.

What is wrong about negligence is that the irresponsible person places someone's welfare in the control of chance. Once that has been done, nobody can influence the outcome. By no stretch of imagination can that procedure be called right or honest, whether it is done intentionally or not.

Consider another situation. If a motorist drives through a crowd of pedestrians, chance decides whether anybody gets killed. The law may penalize him heavily if a death results and lightly if it doesn't, but the wrong is exactly as wrong as when nobody is hurt. If this example seems farfetched, carry it into the next step.

The chance-taker is someone with a habit of taking

chances. If no damage results on one occasion, he feels relatively safe. Consider the game of Russian roulette. The rules are simple. The chance-taker puts one cartridge into a revolver, gives the barrel a spin, points the muzzle at his temple and pulls the trigger, trusting to chance that the cartridge is not in firing position. If it is, he loses his life. If he uses a six-shooter, he has five chances to one of surviving.

Among other things, the law of chance says that if a person keeps taking chances, he will get caught. Therefore, the habitual chance-taker, by the simplest sort of elementary logic, stands convicted as an irresponsible person. He is not safe, and if he controls the welfare of others, they are not safe.

There are other kinds of irresponsibility: failing to live up to obligations and discharge proper duties, dealing with money or figures carelessly, undertaking serious responsibility without proper qualifications, rushing through dangerous episodes without considering possible consequences, failing to give proper attention to people and conditions, permitting needless waste, allowing an inequity to persist or refusing to right a wrong.

Perhaps the most prevalent kind of dishonest irresponsibility is expressed in ordinary conversation.

It is dishonest to handle facts or figures loosely, to make irresponsible statements, to gloss over the dangers of a serious situation, to establish false assumptions as tools of thought, to advance or defend an unsound judgment or position, to employ trickery or chicanery, to be arbitrary or bigoted, to neglect logic or common sense, to compensate for lack of merit by use of pressure, to brush aside mistakes or refuse to admit error, to favor your interests unduly, to make an irresponsible promise, to neglect a responsible promise once made, to blame your troubles on others, to justify yourself and your habits without regard to the facts, to betray a trust, to bear false witness or spread malicious gossip.

One never knows when casual conversation will lead to serious results, and these days there is great need for serious national and international conversations. Unfortunately some of that conversation comes from dishonest, misguided and malicious people. Perhaps the most dangerous persons in our midst are those who argue and plot for irresponsible changes in government policy or economic system or who lead us into traps set by unfriendly nations.

What I am suggesting is no abridgment of free speech; it is a moral rather than a legal consideration. *Remember that freedom of speech also permits freedom of dishonesty in speech.* People had better learn to detect it when they encounter it. The easiest way is for a person to notice his own dishonest thoughts, conversation and conduct.

Honesty is being right instead of wrong in what a person thinks, says and does. Honesty comes from sensitizing the conscience and learning to follow it, and that is an intellectual process.

Dishonesty is using wrong thoughts, words and methods to advance personal motives. Dishonest words and deeds spring out of dishonest and distorted thoughts, and that puts a burden on the honest person to be aware in his mental processes. He should stop impulsively speaking or acting without checking, and he should continue checking until he has acquired habits of intellectual honesty. For the person who aspires to be invulnerable, there is no other way.

In the final analysis, it proves easier to be honest than to be dishonest. *Moreover honesty is the essential key to every other virtue.* Therefore, honesty should head the list of everybody's personal assets. An honest person calculates his remarks and acts so that complete fairness results, avoids risks, makes important decisions responsibly, informs himself as to what is going on and is accountable. He conditions his responses so that right performance becomes natural and instinctive. He cultivates and obeys every incentive he knows is right and has confidence in the result that develops. He gives his honest intent stimulation by espousing right action as it arises in his affairs.

An honest person learns right techniques and masters the pertinent principles in every field where he makes important decisions. When a choice is required, he resorts to honest principles instead of personal choices; principles are impersonal and infallible. He bases decisions on distinctions between right and wrong and stands uncompromisingly on the side of right. He postpones vital decisions until he knows what is right; then he proceeds without hesitation.

Each person should search out examples of inadvertent dishonesty and get the habit of admitting shortcomings and mistakes, especially to himself. He should never pretend nor put up a bluff nor knowingly mislead. He should curb negative urges, control resentment, stay calm, and not act nor speak in anger. He should refuse to reason from his emotional reactions, his pocketbook or desire for selfish gain. He should correct bad habits and stop doing what he thinks is wrong even when alone and unobserved. He should regard temptation as a time to practice self-discipline and train his conscience to stand guard over his behavior. By doing so, he develops a sound resolve against dishonesty in every form.

The kinds of dishonesty under discussion may be difficult to correct, but the person who corrects them takes a long step toward intellectual and emotional maturity. If society has to wait until the average person becomes mature, the present generation should get busy. *It is true that a person gains the full benefits of absolute right only when he has gone the whole way, but it is also true that correcting obvious abuses substantially improves the way his life unfolds.*

Obviously it is wrong and, therefore, dishonest to steal. A person steals when he takes or accepts what is not his, even when he does it without committing an outright theft. That is a broad definition, but in the next lengthy sentence, I am going to make it broader. In essence, it is stealing to do any of the following: gain a reward under false pretense, pay too little for what is received, charge too much for what is sold, sell inferior merchandise to an unsuspecting consumer, keep what is found without seeking the rightful owner, accept or give an actual or implied bribe, fail to pay for damage you caused, unreasonably consume another person's time and attention, pay a worker less than he earns, do less than is paid for, demand what you are not entitled to receive, fail to give proper credit for a suggestion or an intangible benefit, pick a person's mind to appropriate his ideas, defraud by deceit or chicanery, take unfair advantage or unrightfully deprive anybody of a benefit of any sort.

In other words, it is stealing to appropriate an unearned and undeserved item unless, in fact, it is a gift.

It is wrong to steal even for a good cause and equally wrong to accept or buy what someone else has stolen.

If a person thinks I was unduly harsh with the definition of stealing, he should reread the preceding paragraphs and ask how many of those things he would like done to him.

Earlier in this chapter, I discussed the kind of dishonesty that results from carelessness, negligence and irresponsibility. Next I shall discuss the dishonesty of unbridled ambition.

Basically there is nothing wrong with ambition. The world's constructive work is done by ambitious people, but we have to eliminate unbridled ambition. What is wrong about unbridled ambition is that its possessor bases his distinctions between right and wrong on what he thinks will advance or retard his personal aims. He is ambitiously out for himself, and he puts what he considers his profit and advantage ahead of others' welfare. When his self-chosen motives contradict the common good, somebody gets hurt.

His thinking is twisted so that his unbridled ambition seems to justify whatever means he can effectuate.

He may pursue his dishonest ambitions constantly or only occasionally. He may be dishonest in a thousand ways or in only one or two. *To the precise extent a person seems to succeed by dishonesty, he renders his life unsafe.* To the extent that he is dishonest, he succeeds only among dishonest people. If his dishonest acts are frequent, they sentence him to associate with people he cannot trust—a fact he does not learn until after he becomes honest. In the meantime, he is constantly on guard to protect his selfish interests.

Here are examples of unbridled ambition: the customer who boorishly pushes ahead in line, the driver who tries to pass everything ahead of him, the traveler who arrives last but wants to board first, the arguer who insists on having the final word, the bragger who does all the talking and wants all the applause, the victim of inferiority who incessantly discusses his worth, the idea pirate who tries to grab the credit and profit from every joint endeavor, the associate who kills every good idea he did not originate unless he is its prime beneficiary, the fellow worker who advances his career by sacrificing others' interests, the employee who substitutes talk for work, the fawn who flatters the vanity of superiors, the manager who surrounds himself with subordinates tacitly sworn to advance his ambitions despite the general good, the executive who misuses his authority for personal advantage.

A person's unbridled ambition may be observed in any or all such performances. Often he confuses the issue by mixing honesty with his dishonesty, thereby disclosing that he has the capacity for honesty. He would do well to start exercising that capacity all along the line. Even the person who stoops to dishonesty only occasionally is easy to recognize, because his dishonest procedures are transparent to detached observers. They do not take his lapses seriously, partly because they are often guilty of similar lapses and partly because our society is so thoroughly infested with sharp practices that people's sense of honesty is somewhat dulled.

I know persons who are sincerely trying to base their lives on the principle of absolute right, and they testify that their lives are greatly improved as a result. They have discarded the dishonest tactics of unbridled ambition.

People need to learn that only honest right action can bring invulnerability. Then they discover that duty and desire are truly identical, that pursuit of duty brings desired happiness and well-being, and that real freedom comes from thinking, saying and doing what is right. Until that lesson is learned, people continue to have more and more crises and catastrophes.

Clearly the honest person refuses to take or profit by any form of unfair advantage. He drops selfish ambitions and works for the common good. In doing so he discovers the secret of the ages, for he finds that calamity ignores him and visits the person who continues trying to get his own way. He understands that an evildoer can hurt only another doer of evil—a lesson difficult to discern only because so few persons have tested it.

The principle of absolute right is no idle dream. It is based on a natural law. It is practical. I have seen enough people conform to it to know that it is valid. I have also seen people reject it and continue defending their biased definition that right is what favors them. Society has had to set up safeguards to confront those people with resistance. Often such persons meet that resistance by digging in for what they consider self-protection and thus become participants in group dishonesty.

If there is anything more dangerous than individual dishonesty, it is group dishonesty, because group dishonesty leads to organized dishonesty. There are pockets of organized dishonesty everywhere—in governments, unions, business and industry, sports, professions as well as in every criminal activity that infests our social systems.

The purpose of organized dishonesty is to substitute wrong for right. Chicanery, subterfuge, deceit and pressure are used to establish a counterfeit right determined by dishonest leaders to satisfy greed and build or perpetuate dishonest advantage and power. Just as a bribe cannot be effectuated unless there is a taker, organized dishonesty depends on cooperative action. *Organized dishonesty is developed and perpetuated by a network of reciprocal favors, by graft and corruption of officials, but above all, by the support and connivance of dishonest people.*

People don't have to stand for organized dishonesty or allow it to exist. But they do. They countenance and often support it. The dishonest person is rewarded and his dishonesty is made profitable. I know highly respected men, pillars in their churches, who reward dishonest persons by giving them special privilege. In bestowing those privileges they must close their eyes to what they know is wrong.

Occasionally a dishonest person is given the opportunity to amass inordinate wealth. He is promoted for his cleverness, is voted into office, is patronized, and his enterprises made profitable. Thus his dishonesty becomes a source of gain, which encourages others to adopt similar ways to get their share of dishonest profit. Clearly this sort of support for dishonesty should be brought to a halt as quickly as possible.

The truth is that a greater number of average persons should stop supporting or contributing to the success of organized dishonesty in any form, accepting advantages and favors of any dishonest group, becoming members of a pocket of organized dishonesty; and if they find themselves in one, to get out.

There is no use trying to be honest in a den of thieves. It can't be done. A person either succumbs to temptation and makes himself a party to dishonesty or he gets out. When a person sees dishonesty, he should not move over and make room for it. Even loyalty to an employer or spouse does not demand that he support lies and double dealing. If he cannot think of any other remedy, he could change his location.

It is best to do what ought to be done and say what ought to be said to bring dishonest practices out into the open. Dishonesty does not thrive on publicity.

The person with courage to tell the truth in the right way, provided he is not exposing a dishonest group so strongly entrenched that he can be silenced, gets his way. He need only tell his story to people who are honest. When he cannot do that, he can tell it to people who want to be honest. With reasonable support, he can defeat any adversary forced to publicly defend a position that every honest person knows is wrong.

I speak from considerable experience, having investigated many unfair business situations. None of which went uncorrected when the facts came to light.

There is a philosophy of group action that keeps everyone out of trouble. Think, say or do nothing that works against the honest, common good—never neglect the rights of a single person. Seek the decision that is morally right. Every such decision is universally fair, and it automatically serves everybody's proper interests. When a person cannot find that decision, he is not qualified to handle the problem.

Every person has one true standard, and that standard is absolute right.

To reason from another standard is dishonest. No per-

son has a right to expect another to be dishonest. If he succeeds, the other person becomes a part of the conspiracy.
Collaborative or cooperative dishonesty is exactly as wrong
as individual dishonesty, and no one can participate in or
cooperate with dishonesty without being dishonest himself.
In applying this knowledge, everybody is able to suit
everybody, except those who pit their dishonest purposes
against the common good. Nobody can suit them without
becoming a dishonest partner. If a person cannot deal with
someone honestly, he is wise not to deal with that person at
all. When enough people take that attitude, people's dishonesty will become unprofitable in every sense of the word.

Perhaps the most clearly visible sign of organized dishonesty is the constellation of symptoms that surrounds a
pressure group. It was stated previously that pressure is a substitute for facts and usually indicates that somebody is trying
to advance a wrong cause. Pressure by government, industry,
unions, political parties, lobbyists, or any other special interest group is a sign of apprehension to settle an issue on its
merits. **Pressure is once removed from violence, and both
are poor substitutes for honesty.** Everybody should know
that individuals or groups resorting to pressure thereby convict themselves of dishonest intent. At the very least, they
convict themselves of inability to use logic with good effect.

There was a day when virtually all arguments were settled
by pressure and conflict: warfare, duels, kidnapping, murder
and the like. As society became more civilized, courts were
established so that disputes could be settled on their merits.
When an unbiased court handles a dispute intelligently, the
result is good. The courts, however, are also subjected to dishonest pressure and whether they have progressed or retro-
gressed over the years is questionable.

Pressure is not needed to establish a valid point, at least, not when a fair hearing can be had. But is it possible to get a fair hearing on any vital public issue? Procedures for doing it are discussed later, and manifestly they should be applied on a broad scale in our country and everywhere.

Chapter 9

The Importance of Being Right

PRECEDING CHAPTERS stated and inferred numerous reasons why it is important to be right. *Right is what works without detriment of any sort, it encourages other people to get on the side of right, and it serves the best interests of everybody properly involved.* It keeps a person out of trouble and gives him the courage of honest conviction. It provides a virtually infallible rule of conduct that guarantees high ethical standards in every phase of human relations and, in fact, in every phase of life. It brings a person influence, progress, happiness, peace of mind. It draws on his highest faculties and best energies in every decision and every action he takes. It gives him appropriate words for every situation and pulls him through any crisis, but it does more than that. It prevents the occurrence of a crisis resulting from negligence or failure.

The right thing to do is always the best, safest, and most expedient thing to do. When a person is right, he does not have to use force, pressure, pull, scheming or any other artificial method for winning his point. Because right action is to the best advantage of everybody involved, it is easy to facilitate. Doing what is wrong makes a person vulnerable. A wrong decision normally has to be reversed when the facts come to light, whereas a right decision is difficult or impossible to upset.

Many serious crises result from people's conflicts; therefore, this chapter will be devoted to that topic. I am going to discuss group conflict, especially the sort of group conflict that has given us difficult labor relations. But, first, I shall present certain fundamentals that can best be approached by reference to individual conflict.

If pressure is dishonest, so is conflict. Except for outright physical self-defense, conflict is generally a procedure of meeting opposition with wrong. That procedure is indefensible. The reasonable solution for conflict is to meet wrong with right.

Because people trying to be right reason from the same reference points, conflict is not possible until wrong is somehow introduced. Except for solely physical combat, the tools of conflict are dishonesty, harassment, put-downs, slander, insults, such things as those.

The object of fighting is to hurt. Obviously it is wrong to hurt a person, to damage his interests, to injure his reputation, or even to abuse his emotional welfare. It is wrong to be discourteous, malicious, irresponsible, predatory or overly aggressive. It is wrong to create or perpetuate an inequity, to arouse negative emotion, to stimulate a useless controversy, to substitute personal force for logic or to defend a wrong position. It is wrong to hate, nurse a grudge, seek revenge, express anger or jealousy or to let negative emotion supplant intelligence.

What is meant is that it is wrong to start a dispute, wrong to let a dispute start, wrong to keep a dispute alive and let a dispute continue.

Practically all conflicts are caused by injustice or misunderstanding. Conflict starts when somebody is wrong in thought, word or deed. The wrong may be intentional or accidental; it may be real or imagined. *An accidental or imagined wrong can cause as much damage as an intentional wrong, because any wrong is wrong.*

If a person is cautious about preventing what is wrong,

he does not get into conflicts. Instead he gets his life on the right track, and his plans flower and lead to accomplishment. Perhaps his success produces jealousy in others so that jealous persons may try to interfere. A jealous person cannot interfere until he has found an opening. By an opening, I mean a point on which the other person is vulnerable, and the only way to be vulnerable is to be wrong. Until someone is wrong, there is no reason to fight.

It is an old story that it takes two to fight. You may think that the person who does not fight when affronted must take a lot of pushing around. That is not true. Popular assumption seems to be that when a person turns the other cheek, he invites another blow. He doesn't. *The person willing to turn the other cheek does not receive the first blow.* Nobody is tempted to strike him because, on the whole, the person who does not fight does not invite attack. If he knows how to handle his human relations, he neither pushes nor is pushed.

He can win or avoid an argument with any person who is off the track, and he does it by applying the principle of absolute right. He knows that the sure way to defeat wrong is to hold right in contrast to wrong, that honesty defeats dishonesty, and that even a small group of right thinkers can defeat a large group whose might is supported by dishonesty.

People need to learn that the way to persuade is not to judge that an opponent is an adversary and then launch an attack. There are better ways. Start by giving yourself an objective viewpoint. *Do not oppose a person; instead, oppose only what is wrong. Dislike what he says, if you must, but do not dislike him. Recognize that it is not necessary to fight for right—only to state it.* Set into motion the forces of corrective action by recognizing and speaking the truth. *No person can long withstand the continued onslaught of carefully presented truth. It will finally compel recognition of error. It will finally reconcile the causes of misunderstanding and correct what is wrong.*

When a person engages in a fight, it is an admission that he has not learned a better way to manage his interpersonal affairs. But there are stronger reasons for avoiding conflict, and I shall express them in elementary terms.

If an opponent can be defeated, there is no need to fight. If he cannot be defeated, fighting is foolish. Unless a person is careful, he finds that he takes a licking even in the process of defeating an opponent. Despite these truths, the average person finds himself engaged in conflict at frequent intervals.

There is a sequence to every conflict that is duplicated monotonously every day all over the earth. Few persons understand that sequence, but the person who does, so far as his own life is concerned, puts a stop to conflict.

Conflict can be stopped before it starts and after it starts. It can be stopped at any step. Either adversary can stop it by simply resorting to friendly and honest responses rather than unfriendly and dishonest reactions. The first one to stop the conflict shows himself to be enlightened.

The situation of conflict arises when a person gives offense. That is most likely to happen after someone else invited offense, but conflict does not materialize until offense is taken. *Here, then, is the formula to prevent conflict: Don't give offense; don't invite offense; don't take offense.*

The easy way to give offense is to make trouble for somebody, and the easy way to make trouble is to think, say or do what is wrong. Maybe it is only emotional trouble that is caused, but emotional trouble is what produces conflict. Maybe it is only another person's wrongness that invites someone to make trouble, but the person who is wrong needs help rather than to be attacked. That help is given by aiming high instead of low when dealing with people.

Look for a way to reduce trouble, not to increase it.

One summer day while entertaining friends, including my boss, my wife and I wanted to make favorable impressions, but the unexpected happened.

The boss, resplendent in a white suit, picked up a wide smear of green paint from a garden chair. I saw it happen, saw him notice it, and tried to restrain my panic as he muttered a quiet word of chagrin. Then without attracting attention from the other guests, he got up and started toward the house.

Hurriedly, I followed. When I caught up, he realized I knew of his predicament. At once the response of a good friend came forth, "I'm certainly glad that happened to me and not someone else."

The person who does not take offense never gets into fights. The person who tries to conduct his relationships on that basis does not get into fights. As will be discussed later, trying is virtually equal to succeeding.

Long experience has demonstrated that there are times when a person has to resist sudden temptation: to react to a slur with a scornful retort, to puncture someone's ego, deflate him and put him down. Often that can be done so that bystanders laugh and applaud. But take out the rush of ideas to bring laughter and applause, and what is left is rather ugly. The scornful retort upsets the other person's reason, causing him to behave in a belligerent manner so that the sequence of conflict is then in full swing. Conflict is avoided by understanding treatment from either or both participants.

A popular fallacy has it that when a person is struck, he is entitled to strike back. The fact is every blow invites a stronger blow. Immediately each opponent must get even, and his idea of getting even is to hurt his opponent more than he was hurt. The thrusts and counterthrusts may fall in rapid succession or may be as widely spaced as the moves in a chess game played by mail.

There is only one outcome. The conflict runs its full course until one antagonist gains sufficient advantage that he loses interest, loses his nerve and retreats, or is dead. In other words it continues until one antagonist believes he has won and the other has lost.

Fighting is no way to settle a moral issue. In fact, it is an invitation to the less scrupulous antagonist to do his worst. In addition, each thrust and counterthrust invites bad feeling. Even when a person is right at the outset, indignation and temper soon cloud the mind. There is no such thing as truly righteous indignation, for when a person loses his temper, rationality goes along. The next step is to meet wrong with wrong, and to that extent, a person becomes vulnerable. After that, personal force is needed to carry his cause, and that cannot be done in the face of honest opposition. Therefore, what is called for is a return to rationality.

The sensible procedure is to break off the conflict and let right prevail. Either antagonist can do it. When it is done, the antagonist who is wrong finds his position undermined. Rightness wins the point.

Recently I was driving through an unfamiliar town in heavy traffic, searching for a certain side street. Consequently I stayed to the extreme right and passed three consecutive streets before I found my turn. A patrol car pulled up beside me and forced me to the curb. I got out and approached the policeman. "Evidently I did something wrong," I said.

"You can say that again," he grumbled. "Let me see your license!"

While producing it, I took my time so I could think about what I might say. "Let me explain what I was doing," I said, "and I think you'll understand. I was looking for the Y.M.C.A., and I knew it was off to the right on one of the streets I passed. Perhaps you thought I was trying to pass traffic on the right."

The officer's attitude underwent a complete change. He became friendly and helpful. In a few words he told me where to find the Y.M.C.A., apologized, and we parted friends.

What this story illustrates is that the person who is taking right action needs only to state his case. In dealing with any fair-minded person, he gets what he should without argument.

The only time such tactics do not cause right to prevail is when wrong is deeply entrenched or strongly organized. Then a person needs support from a judge and jury honest enough to see that right purposes are served. Telling the truth does it, and the response is much like what happens when a hungry crowd is called to dinner. Failure occurs only when a person cannot get a hearing from honest people.

With the foregoing as a preliminary, let us devote the next few pages to the topic of conflict in labor relations.

Often I have had to settle disputes between industrial workers and management. There is only one procedure I have ever followed: Talk to the key individuals, and get everybody's complete story. While each person is blowing off his emotional steam, collect all the facts. Find out what is right and what is wrong in the situation. Find ways to prove what is right or wrong. With that knowledge, get all the individuals to recognize and correct errors in their thinking. As a result, only one answer has ever emerged, and it is an answer that is acceptable to everybody.

By using that procedure, I have never had to act as judge or jury, never had to pose as attorney for the prosecution or defense, never had to arbitrate, and never had to enforce a decision. Every decision was arrived at voluntarily and enforced itself by unanimous mutual consent.

The foregoing routine was applied hundreds of times to hundreds of problems with no exception in the result.

A dispute starts when a person, perhaps more than one, is wrong. It is corrected only when those who are wrong become right. There is a key point that makes every decision easy: A person instinctively wants to do what he knows is right. If that statement seems incorrect, it is only because few persons have had the opportunity or patience to go through such analyses themselves. After having seen that routine work consistently, I have complete confidence in it.

Of course, any dispute is somewhat confusing at first. Perhaps there are as many sides as participants and many fallacious arguments. But underlying all the verbiage there is a thread of basic truth that is convincing to everybody once it is exposed. Seldom must a person expose it himself. By asking intelligent questions, the truth gradually is brought out.

If anyone hampers another's progress toward what is right, his embarrassment can progressively be increased until he is willing to face truth. If he resists what is reasonable, he can be asked, "Do you want to do what is right?" I have met many people whose emotions were difficult to manage but none who was willing to answer by saying no.

I have learned that few disputes are settled by others with the procedure just described. In many disputes, no effort is made to collect all the facts. Instead, disputes are won by the disputants able to exert greatest pressure and are lost by the disputants who lack strategic advantage. *The truth is a dispute should not be won or lost; it should be resolved. That is accomplished by the direct application of honesty.*

No participant in conflict is likely to accept the fact that conflict is resolved by the simple application of honesty on both sides. But it is true. The reason is that conflict grows out of intentional or unintentional dishonesty and cannot thrive unless the dishonesty is allowed to persist. Unconsciously each side tends to perpetuate its dishonest stance.

The simplest way to resolve group conflict is to bring in a truly impartial mediator whose objective is to see that the facts become clear to everybody involved. His job is to see that right prevails, and that is his only job. To do that, he must expose error, exaggeration, misunderstanding, false statements and truth. He does it without stating any issue under dispute, leaving that to the disputants themselves. It often helps to ask questions: *"Are you trying to do the right thing?" "Will you accept the right answer when it emerges?"* Such questions impel disputants to declare their intention to be fair.

Similarly statements of principle generate fairness and confidence: *"When the right answer is found, it will suit everybody involved." "The person who makes a mistake needs help more than he needs to be hurt."*

A true mediator never takes sides. If he does, he adds pressure to what the opposing side thinks it must defeat. No longer is he a mediator; he is party to the dispute.

I have used the foregoing procedures for settling numerous labor disputes, involving unions and companies known to be tough. After emotions cooled, never have they failed to bring a satisfactory solution to everybody involved. The reason is twofold: An impartial questioner discloses information that shows error whether it results from misunderstanding or from intent; second, almost nobody will openly convict himself of being dishonest. He is not willing to say, "I know I'm wrong, but I insist on my point anyhow."

Those principles refer to labor disputes, and the same principles apply to negotiation of most labor contracts.

With contracts, the dispute is artificial in nature. It does not arise from a local situation of real or imagined wrongness, injustice or misunderstanding as in the case of a dispute between a worker and his foreman. Instead, one side sets up demands and the other side sets up resistance, resulting in conflict that is almost always settled on the basis of pressure. The conflict could be resolved by exposing what is right and letting it prevail—so long as the disputants' representatives are willing to be honest.

Sometimes an honest result is not acceptable to all the representatives' constituents, and then it has to be regarded as a "mutually unsatisfactory" result. I have seen that sort of result develop more than once, and it is the only concession that is morally right, because it is a concession to honesty.

The trouble is that people seldom employ collective bargaining procedures that achieve the kind of honest settlement described in these pages.

Some persons may scoff at that statement. "What about fact-finding committees?" they may ask. The answer is that even when the fact finders are right, a fact-finding committee ordinarily is used for exerting pressure. That pressure is resisted by everybody in a position to resist.

"What about impartial umpires?" may be another question. The answer is that an umpire makes a binding decision, which a fact-finding committee usually cannot, and as a result, it is virtually impossible to get an umpire appointed. The disputants are seldom willing to surrender use of their pressure tactics.

"What about arbitrators?" may be a third question. The answer to that question is more complicated to explain. It is my observation that an arbitrator too often is one who makes an arbitrary decision. He tries to give a piece of the victory to each contestant on the theory that if each gets a concession the arbitrator may be hired again.

His usual function is to mark out the area of a dispute at

the time he enters it; then he finds some way to give mutually satisfactory concessions until no dispute remains. Thus contradictory pressure finally decides the outcome, and the arbitrator is only a shock reducer. What is right rarely has anything to do with the outcome.

A right decision is not reached by appeasement, by horse-trading, by compromise or by concessions. It is reached by exposing the facts and letting them control. It must be done in a way that enables each disputant to recognize the facts for himself. They cannot be jammed into the mind of a person who is so excited he cannot distinguish right from wrong.

I think that conventional procedures for settling labor disputes are wrong. I hold that when every party to a dispute is properly represented and all the facts are clear in everybody's mind, the right decision goes with the facts. Only when one or more of the disputants is willing to be publicly dishonest and to seek support for his dishonesty do decisions go wrong.

Several years' experience with both unions and management and with executives and labor convinces me that the foregoing program is entirely practical. And that it is not just an ivory-tower dream. I have been involved in many labor disputes and numerous negotiations of labor contracts, and every one of them was settled in the manner described.

Everybody needs to know that the most important thing in this world is to be right. The second most important thing is to get others to be right also.

Right can always be defended, can hardly be criticized, can seldom be overruled. But wrong makes you vulnerable, undermines the strength of your position, invites others to knock you down, and provides the very tools for doing it.

The benefit of right thought and right action is limitless. The penalty of wrong thought and wrong action is destruction. A person who lives by the principle of absolute right bears a charmed life. When a person gets on the wrong track, life becomes complicated and impossible to manage; but when he is on the right track, his activities succeed. It is as simple as it sounds.

I have cited enough benefits to assure that it is wise to be right, but I have saved the greatest benefit until last.

Earlier it was stated that conforming to the principles of absolute right enables a person always to do what he wants to do to the exclusion of doing what he does not want to do. Perhaps that seemed to be a selfish philosophy. It is. But at the same time, it is wholly unselfish—which seems contradictory until the meanings of those two words are understood.

Right is an exact quality, and on every basic issue, there is an identity between what benefits the individual and what benefits humanity as a whole. When people learn to reconcile selfishness with unselfishness, we will have our better world. The perfect way of accomplishing that reconciliation is to conform to the principle of absolute right.

Surely that must be the meaning of the admonition, "Love thy neighbor as thyself." Love not more nor less, but as *thyself.*

Right and expediency are identical. So are right and might. So are unselfishness and selfishness. The person who comprehends those truths is the one who improves our world by improving his own. He always has plenty of interesting and productive things to do, because the opportunity to do what is right is in bountiful supply in our world today. *To do what is right, therefore, is the natural formula for having a spectacular career and fulfilling existence.*

Chapter 10

How To Make an Honest Decision

THIS CHAPTER presents an approach to right thinking that many persons will find helpful in opening dramatic opportunities. Of all the concepts in this book, what follows is most likely to be thought controversial. It is open to skepticism on the ground that its validity is not confirmed by the average person's experience. There are two ways to confirm its validity: one is to check its logic, and the other is to put it to use and gain that experience.

Previously I asserted that the sum total of a person's duty is to think, speak and act in conformity with the principle of right because it is based on a natural law: ***right action gets right results; wrong action gets wrong results.*** I asserted that the person who bases decisions on distinctions between right and wrong does what he wants to do, because then there is an identity between what he wants to do and what is right.

His life is protected, and in this chapter, it will be shown that sincere intent to do what is right is all that is required. ***The average person does not know that freedom of choice consists of the ability conscientiously to think, say and do what is right.*** In this nation, people are allowed to exercise that freedom, and the only time they lose it is when they do what is wrong. Few persons know that, consequently few take advantage of that freedom.

People are restrained by fearful thoughts, so they think they dare not quit their jobs, although many would be wise to branch out for themselves. They think they dare not engage in competition, although many would find they have no competition. They think they dare not speak their minds, although they would find that truth cannot be assailed. They think they dare not act on honest purposes, although they would discover that honest purposes succeed.

When making decisions, the average person fails to ask himself what is right. Instead he asks himself what would please him. He thinks with his pride, his prejudices, his pocketbook. When selfish ambition is the basic ingredient of a decision, he gets a wrong answer, leading to a wrong result. Despite the wrongness of that result, he may set out to prove his decision was right. That explains how a person gets into much of his trouble.

Freedom of choice implies ability to make voluntary decisions, but that ability is hedged in by a vital restriction. The individual should not act on wrong decisions. *Every question has many possible wrong answers and only one answer that is right.* To the person who lives by absolute right, the right question determines the right answer. The right answer is predestined. Asking the right question, therefore, is vital and leads to another illuminating discovery.

A complicated problem is not solved readily until the problem is captured in an accurately stated question. Often the question so clearly predestines the answer that the answer is obvious at once. Just as the right question predestines the right answer, the problem predestines the right question.

The problem predetermines the question, and the question predetermines the answer. Therefore, the sequence begins with the problem and not with the question.

Suppose, for example, a house were on fire. That would constitute a problem, and it would give rise to several questions. In one way or another, those questions would concern what to do. Several answers in combination would be right. Call the fire department, save whatever valuables you rightly can, start fighting the fire and so on, depending on conditions. But the facts of the fire and the local conditions determine both the questions and the answers.

What this means is that realistically a person does not *make* a decision. Instead, he *finds* it. He collects, analyzes, and interprets the facts. Those facts are captured in correctly worded questions. Then the answers are found. The decision is the result. By following correct procedure, any two persons in the same situation get the same decision.

The foregoing example provides a principle, a universal truth: **Right decisions are found, not made.** The principle applies to every problem no matter how complicated, although often it may be difficult to trace out in detail.

In the field of human relations, for example, that principle is only the confirmation of an earlier statement that when handling labor problems, it is essential to find the facts and assure that they control. The person who accepts the reality of the principle and allows for it discovers a vast improvement in the management of any problems he is called on to solve.

Every right answer is determined by a right question, and every right question is determined by correct interpretation of a problem.

Seemingly the sequence of analysis begins with a problem, but only for a person who lets his problems be selected by the vicissitudes of life. Such a person is not truly free; his problems, questions, and answers (if effectively handled) are predetermined by factors beyond his control. The way to escape and gain freedom from such problems is to select project problems. As many successful inventors or creative thinkers have learned, that creates a rewarding occupation.

There is a simple procedure for converting the foregoing paragraphs into action. Constantly search out important project problems, and capture them on paper in specific form as a normal part of living.

When the opportunity arises, select one for treatment. Select the problem project you think you can handle: environmental, social, political, or relationship problem. Be sure that the selection combines complete selfishness with complete unselfishness. Convert the project problem into the question that is dictated by it, then convert the question into its correct answer. Enough persons doing that repeatedly would change the world.

In following the foregoing procedure, a person never has confusion over what to do next. He gradually discovers that his life begins expressing a natural plan. To others his life may look extremely complicated, but to him it looks simple. He sees a clear path of action stretching ahead that makes sense, therefore, he follows it.

That procedure gives anybody's path of life a high degree of purposeful strength. People who might seek to deter or dissuade may consider such persons stubborn perhaps, which only shows their lack of similar understanding. Anyone who finds the perfect formula that combines maximum self-interest with maximum service to others could not be dissuaded nor deterred.

The fact is that in the ideal life there is an identity between selfishness and unselfishness; therefore, by implication, there is an identity between predestination and free will.

By exercising his freedom of choice, the individual unerringly follows the path of action that is best for him and for humanity as a whole. In the final analysis, that is what determines his choice. In doing so he achieves a grand predestination in his affairs by working from an assumption that his will is free. He also discovers what freedom really means: *The person who chooses to be right is free, and any other so-called freedom actually is a form of unsuspected slavery.* That slavery is explained in later pages.

Perhaps the strongest point expressing the concept of free will is the individual's consciousness of freedom to make choices. Because serious thinkers, through the centuries, have argued the subject of predestination versus free will, I shall devote the next few pages to its consideration.

Consciousness is the awareness of our surroundings. It is also the ability to remember and to deal in abstract concepts. *Perhaps consciousness serves its highest function in relation to decisions, and arriving at a right decision is perhaps the best example of a free will at work.*

If the will were not free, why would a person need to be conscious? If decisions were automatic, why would he need any more consciousness than a calculator? Surely consciousness is not provided merely so that people could enjoy and suffer. Instead, *consciousness epitomizes people's ability to discern choices in the practical situations of life. In a very real sense, consciousness is the stuff of life.*

The person who decides to live under an assumption that his will is free is, from that moment, conscious of freedom. He increases that consciousness of freedom by exercising it.

Soon he discovers that free functioning of his conscious ability to choose what is right brings whatever he needs. He discovers that money and material things are as free as water and air, and that only self-applied restrictions in the past use of his freedom have denied him what he needed. From this, a person can deduce that feelings of frustration are a sign that he is not exercising his freedom.

Consciousness is evidence of free will and evidence of opportunity to make free choices. Therefore, it is evidence of the ability to choose between right and wrong. He who chooses wrong loses his freedom. That information narrows freedom of choice; only the choice of right will do. Therefore, people are free to choose right but not wrong. Thus consciousness is limited so that only the right thinker perpetuates and extends his freedom.

Freedom is the opportunity to choose what is right. If life is viewed as an unceasing series of problem situations, then freedom is the opportunity to get the right answers. When life is conducted in accordance with a long series of right decisions, that has the effect of giving life a perfect destiny.

The destiny is not necessarily fixed in advance, for one wrong decision destroys that destiny, and then a new one is established. The destiny is an ideal rather than a literal predetermination. It represents the individual's path of perfect opportunity, and if he finds and acts on right decisions all along the line, he fulfills life's destiny for him.

Once a person sees the reasoning behind those concepts, he tends to absorb them into his pattern of life.

Some things are predestined by nature such as the fact that the morning sun appears on the eastern horizon or that winter follows autumn. But a person often takes a hand in destiny himself. He may take action that predestines, for example, the time of his death, he may toss a ball into the air and predestine its return to earth, or predestine his size by the amount and kind of food he eats. It is a matter of cause and effect. Establish a natural cause, and the effect arises in due course.

If life is a series of choices in accordance with the principle of absolute right, then each person has a perfect path of life stretching out before him. Given the opportunity, his life plans itself.

What if he gets off the right track?

If he does, the same is true. He continues to experience an unending series of opportunities for right choices. His path may be different, but it will still be a perfect path. His task is to find it. Unless his wandering involves irrevocable damage, all he loses is time. That loss in itself is irrevocable, but it does not necessarily change the nature of his future. His perfect future is found by getting on the right track and staying there.

It is a human tendency to believe in detailed planning. People are instructed and encouraged to set goals and work out plans for achieving them. To achieve the perfect life, people do not need detailed blueprints made up in advance. In fact, to set a goal becomes more than a device for achieving that goal. It becomes a device for causing any other goal to be inadmissible. There may be other goals more useful and inspiring. Few persons of greatness have claimed they planned it all in their youth.

I have shown that the person who constantly searches for opportunities, who at each new step selects the most important opportunity for treatment, and who then makes right choices surrenders his destiny to natural forces. He should check his decisions with common sense as he goes along, but in doing so, his common sense may get some shocks. He finds that **nature is a better planner than a person.**

He discovers that he knows what to do next, has whatever abilities and facilities he needs, and finds they come with little or no forethought on his part. Every person who tries the life of right choices accumulates his own proof of those assertions and concludes that nature is a more vital force than he supposed.

He soon realizes that this world's troubles result from the fact that people try to conduct their lives as though they were omniscient and sometimes omnipotent. Thereafter he is content to entrust his destiny to a power higher than himself, knowing that incessant right choices will lead him wherever he should go. He has no qualms about the future.

For me, the preceding information settles the age-old argument over predestination and free will. But whether the will is free is a somewhat academic question. The answer makes little practical difference, though what a person thinks is the answer makes a great deal of difference. What he thinks determines his conduct. If he thinks he can be of service to others and to himself by exercising his free will, he will exercise it.

While the foregoing pages may be considered controversial, the reason for including them is that they could help readers to aim toward high accomplishment with sufficient confidence to hurdle the obstacles.

What is coming next, I think, is not controversial.

The purpose of this chapter is to show how decisions should be made. It helps to know that *decisions are predetermined by relevant facts.* It is also necessary to have a sound procedure for collecting and understanding those facts. The next few pages will discuss such a procedure.

The first step is to determine when a decision is appropriate. In that connection it helps to recognize that the average person seldom makes a complicated decision until he is driven to it. He lets most decisions go by default, and that is true whether the benefits would be his or society's as a whole. In addition, most of the average person's decisions are based on impulse rather than reasoning. No matter what is said, he continues doing it that way.

Fortunately impulse is frequently as good a basis for action as reasoning if certain considerations are observed.

When a decision is demanded, it should not be neglected. If the facts are clearly understood and the decision falls within the individual's normal scope of operation, an impulsive decision will suffice. An impulsive decision is readily checked for accuracy, and the habit of checking it can be made instinctive. The procedure for doing it is simple: *Determine that the decision is based on an honest impulse in touch with reality.*

For the most part, only the reason behind the decision is vital. Find that reason and inspect it. If it is what the situation calls for, the decision will be honest. If it is honest, it will be right.

To check the honesty of a decision, consider these questions: Does the decision disregard others' rights? Does it contradict duty to self? Does it truly satisfy the best interests of all persons properly involved? To check the honesty of the action based on the decision, try this question: Will the action benefit me, others, or a combination of everybody involved? An honest answer to that question often inspires an improvement in the decision at once.

Wrong decisions are based on false premises or on dishonest personal motives. A decision calculated to effectuate wrong invariably leads to wrong results. That is true if the decision is based on a desire to appear smart, get even, take unfair advantage, to hurt, or to do anything else classified as dishonest in Chapter 8. *Honest decisions made in conformity with the principles of right behavior will necessarily be right.*

No person who is careless, irresponsible, slipshod or thoughtless in approaching problems can expect to get right decisions. Nor can a person whose motives and habits of thought are biased. But everyone becomes both cautious and unbiased when he starts thinking in terms of absolute right. He solves his problems on the basis of simple distinctions between right and wrong, because he perceives those distinctions. When he experiments by dealing with problems within his scope of experience, he finds that he is virtually infallible. Then he discovers that he can extend his virtual infallibility to other areas of his life.

He should intend to be right in all his big and little decisions. An easy way to approach that degree of right intent is to espouse right moral causes in daily affairs. Gradually life itself assumes the nature of a right moral cause. That will bring help of the most valuable sort from other people who also are trying to be right.

What has already been explained simplifies most of life's decisions to a point of understandability. There are, however, certain complicated problems that will be discussed next.

At first glance, some problems appear easy to solve while others appear difficult. *A difficult problem is difficult only when a person is not able to manage it readily. If he keeps trying to understand the problem, it will become easy.* He starts by locating the essential points, making them so obvious and clear that any unbiased observer or listener would agree with them. By the time a person has done that with every essential point, the problem becomes as easy to handle as multiplying numbers, and he feels assured of the correctness of the result.

Consider the worker who must decide whether to resign his position and go into business for himself. Consider the executive who must decide whether or not to fire a subordinate. Consider the great public problems that must be solved by our national leaders. All those problems could be handled in the manner described.

Often it is said that there is no such thing as a perfect solution to any problem. Suppose the problem is to put a car in a garage, to arrive on time for an appointment, to add a column of figures? Suppose the problem is to find the sum of one and one? The answer is two. Could Einstein do better?

There is a perfect solution to every ordinary problem,

and the task is to find it. To accomplish that task, the analyses must be simple and understandable.

The way to be right is to collect and interpret the appropriate facts. Get them all. Then making a decision is only a matter of defining the problem, putting it into the form of a question, and finding the answer to the question. The procedures of arithmetic really tell the story.

Every problem should be reduced to the simplest degree of understandability. Until it is, no person is qualified to deal with it. In addition, if other people's welfare depends on the outcome, attempting to do so shows irresponsibility.

Here is a procedure that embodies the foregoing suggestions: 1. Recognize your problems as they arise, record them on paper, arrange them in sequence of importance, and give them treatment in a systematic manner. 2. Reduce each problem to one or more specific questions that allow for every vital fact, then improve their wording until they define the problem exactly. 3. Collect all the facts, principles, ideas and other pertinent data that are needed to answer the questions, and discard the rest. 4. Combine, rearrange, organize, and simplify the data until the combination that arouses greatest confidence is found. 5. Convert that combination into a specific plan of action and execute it.

Some persons may think I have oversimplified the procedure of making a decision. Many decisions, they may say, are more complicated than that. Not the vital decisions. It is years since life has confronted me with any decision more complicated than the average bridge hand. While my bridge decisions are not vital, I attach great significance to every decision that may alter the course of my life. Those decisions, I have found, are simple when one's intent is to think, say and do what is right.

Some choices are absolute, as is a choice between right

and wrong. When a person faces such a choice, it should be made without equivocation. But other choices are between good and bad, and some are between bad and worse. The basis of those choices is a standard of comparison. The standard of comparison is illustrated by the markings on a ruler or on the scale of a thermometer. The average person makes up his own scale ordinarily, but he should adopt a scale made up from life.

An existing standard may provide a suitable basis from which to work, but if a person wants a method that is better, quicker, cheaper or fairer, for example, he has to measure comparative values. The better method should be adopted, and it should be the best method that can be found. Above all, it should be an honest method with the distinctions between right and wrong that are clear-cut.

When a person gets an answer that gives him confidence from the moral viewpoint, he is invulnerable to trouble. Either he has that confidence or he does not. When he doesn't, he needs further analysis and experiment. When in doubt, it is best for him to continue cautious analyzing. Nobody should take an irrevocable step until he knows he is safe. That procedure protects the best interests of everybody involved, and it constitutes a good definition of honesty in handling important problems.

At this point, I am going to add a touch of philosophy.

There is a giant sleeping within the average person that is a genius. Perhaps the average person thinks he cannot do much to increase his intelligence as such, but he can increase his honesty and get much the same result. Thus he awakens the sleeping giant which gives him the effect of genius, too.

A genius is a person who knows how to be right. That makes all his decisions sound.

Several times in foregoing pages, I have indicated that the individual is capable of virtual infallibility. I have said that the intent to be right is virtually equal to the actuality, and next I shall explain those assertions.

A person should expect a perfect performance from himself and be disappointed when he doesn't get it. Too often the average person shrugs off mistakes with a remark to the effect that it is human to err. Too often he denies or defends his mistakes. That attitude is an invitation to self-deception.

The fact is that a person cannot be totally accurate in all details of his thoughts and speech. He cannot be perfect in all he does. His job is to be right as comprehensively as he can, and there is no more that anyone can do. He cannot afford to be slipshod about trying. Every time he excuses, denies or defends a mistake, he paves the way to additional mistakes of the same kind. Those mistakes fall into categories, built up by a long series of excuses, denials and defenses. Nobody should kid himself about that.

Once a habitual mistake is discovered, it is easy to correct, and the correction puts an end to that series of mistakes.

While it is true that a person cannot be perfect in every detail of his thoughts and their expression, he can be right in the fundamentals. When he is right in the fundamentals, which means when he is honest about every consideration that comes along, surprising results develop.

He finds that life does not demand perfection. *A person does not have to be perfect to get the effect of perfection.* That may seem like a strange concept, but it stands up under analysis.

When a person is dealt a bridge hand, he is confronted with the need to make a decision. He must pass or make a bid on which he will shortly stand or fall. That kind of situation seldom arises in life. Usually the process of making a decision can be protected by preliminaries so managed that they cause no irrevocable harm. A person can adjust and readjust his actions as he proceeds. By constantly edging himself in the direction of what is right and checking himself at frequent intervals, he stays out of trouble.

Other people, seeing his intent to do what is right, tend to make allowances for any mistakes that may occur. Unless they have wrong motives, they help him to stay on the right track.

The right solution to any problem is one that is honest, fair and satisfactory to every person involved, and in reaching that solution, there is usually adequate margin for unintentional error.

Nature has tolerance for well-meaning mistakes: A scrape or cut heals itself. That same tolerance is shared by every right-thinking person. It is read on every blueprint of a manufactured product: The parts do not have to be perfect but must only fall within the required fraction of an inch. If they do, that is acceptable. To all intents and purposes, the product is perfect.

Approaching the solution of a problem is somewhat analogous to the situation of a ferryboat entering its slip. The boat may approach from upstream or down, it may be pointed toward dead center or off to one side, it may scrape against the pilings on either side, it may move slowly or at maximum safe speed. If necessary adjustments are made during the process of docking it, the boat eventually assumes the right position so that proper mechanical couplings are made.

Ordinarily the ferryboat pilot must be clumsy indeed to get into trouble. The same is true of everybody in virtually all the ordinary situations he faces.

The person who gets into frequent trouble is someone who is not trying to do what is right. His mind is on getting his way, and that takes his thinking off the track. His task is to stop trying to get his way and instead to find the right track and stay on it. Then no matter what his past mistakes, so long as none is irrevocable, his life begins to straighten out. He is wise to correct any past mistakes or, at least, to compensate for them when he can. That lets him forget them, and his life becomes blameless and free.

Chapter 11

The Great Cost of Being Wrong

IN MANY persons' minds, the impression prevails that dishonesty can be made profitable. If this book accomplishes its purpose, it will correct that impression. ***Dishonesty benefits nobody. At best, it is a trick for obtaining something of seeming value in exchange for what is priceless.***

It is easy for a person to believe he has gained by taking wrong action. If he conducts a successful burglary, for example, he can spend the proceeds on whatever he wants. He can do the same with profits from any dishonest action if he is not caught. No doubt about that. But there are other ways to get what a person wants, involving less risk. Occasionally books are written by criminals who have made that discovery by turning honest.

Most people would like to believe that wrong action that violates the law doesn't pay, but despite its logic, there are some who scoff. "I know a dishonest man," one may say, "whose dishonesty made him rich. While his victims struggle financially, he thumps his chest and brags about how smart he is. What can be said about that?"

There are three things to say. First, ordinarily nobody can cheat persons who are honest; dishonest persons profit by appealing to somebody's cupidity. Second, dishonest persons cut themselves off from the good life in ways already explained. If they live long enough, the quicksands of dishonesty swallow them. Third, it is almost universally agreed that a person's success is due to what is right about his methods rather than what is wrong. The fact that people mix wrong with right only shows how much further they could have deviated in their quest for profitable advantage.

Invariably the wrongdoer is one of his victims. Seldom does he realize it, and because of that fact, he is led astray by a gigantic delusion. Seldom is he resentful over his own misdeeds, but when he is their victim, he deeply resents the misdeeds of others. First, he must admit *he* is in trouble, and for that reason, he should turn the tables and consider his own misdeeds. That is what I propose to demonstrate in this chapter.

Words and deeds are under control of the brain. Therefore, the wrongdoer is a wrong thinker. *No matter how successful he appears to be, the wrong thinker is a slave to his wrongness.* He makes many plans that cannot work out. He is torn between duty and desire. His life is filled with tension and internal friction. He cannot achieve identity between selfishness and unselfishness. He can rarely do as he pleases. To meet the requirements of life, he must often do what he would rather avoid.

One of his problems is that other people tend to deprive him of opportunities. When honest people get his number, they ignore or frustrate him. Honest people do not associate with him on free and easy terms, and usually they tactfully conceal that fact from him. There are individuals who go through life as failures because they have thus destroyed other people's confidence in them, and most of them never know why.

Intent to be honest permits easy detection of dishonesty in others. Figuratively it destroys the blinders on a person's eyes so that he can identify a dishonest person by the way he runs a business, the way he deals with people and manages his personal affairs. There are people who have been so habitually dishonest that a discerning stranger can read the evidence in their faces and demeanor. That is a high price to pay for questionable gain.

It is possible to recognize dishonesty in a person's conversation by the contradictions he voices. It is recognized in exhibitions of jealousy, expressions of self-aggrandizement, attitudes of resentment or defense, efforts to conceal motives and displays of aggression.

The dishonest person is likely to invite disputes and to have trouble in getting them settled. Therefore, one of the penalties of dishonesty is a succession of arguments, controversies and conflicts.

Along with inviting disputes, the dishonest person makes wrong decisions, having adverse effects on the interests of others. However, when the facts come to light, a wrong decision practically compels its own correction. *The way to avoid wrong decisions is to adopt the intent to be right, and the way to do that is to be honest.*

Conscience must be brought into full play. It must be sensitized and used. There is no such thing as too much honesty nor too much conscience.

The drive of conscience is emotional. The person who disregards that drive may think he can somehow nullify its force. He cannot. The force will exert itself somewhere, and unless it is used as nature intended, the result is harmful.

The person who tries to ignore his conscience is constantly confused between duty and desire. Consequently he suffers endless frustration and inner conflict that undermines his emotional well-being.

The fully honest person is emotionally secure. He withstands emotional strains. He lives without fear. *His intent to think, say and do what is right makes him invulnerable to other people's trouble, and he doesn't cause trouble for himself.*

A generation ago, almost any doctor would have scoffed at

the idea that physical illness has emotional origins. Today many of them agree that a large proportion of sicknesses have emotional origins. That conclusion is confirmed by several formerly sickly persons of my acquaintance who have learned to satisfy the promptings of conscience and regained their health.

It is a tired joke that the person who needs a doctor has something wrong with him, and the person who needs a psychiatrist ought to have his head examined. But the evidence is that when people learn to be honest, their doctors become less overworked.

Such are the emotional and physical problems of dishonesty, and the benefits of the person who cleanses his mind of wrong thoughts.

Earlier I stated that conscious guilt tends to alter a person's conduct and demeanor so that his dishonesty is observable. Though harder to detect, unconscious guilt is just as obvious to the discerning eye.

Unconscious guilt results from dishonest thinking, dishonest words, and dishonest action. Dishonest thinkers are persons who blame other people for their troubles, because they fail to recognize it is *their* thoughts and emotions that lead to *their* wrong results and trouble. *Dishonest thinkers have difficulty distinguishing right thoughts from wrong thoughts; consequently they have no easy method for solving problems. Unless they change, they are destined to spend their days in confusion without understanding the cause.*

The fact that a person behaves intelligently does not mean that he is intelligent, and the fact that he behaves stupidly does not mean that he is stupid. The average person often does both. Every normal person, whether he behaves stupidly or not, is intelligent. He has the same mental faculties as his contemporaries.

I have high regard for what the average person could do, but low regard for what he actually does; it is often far inferior to what he could do. He fails to utilize the benefit of his intelligence, and that is important to society, because it determines how he handles his obligations and responsibilities. It is equally important to him, because it determines how he handles his personal affairs. Beyond those considerations, it also determines the esteem in which he is held by others. Their judgments of his character and ability are based on his actual performance—not on what he could or should do.

The remainder of this chapter expresses the concept that caused me to decide years ago that ultimately I would write this book.

It is seldom noticed, but dishonesty is a way of seeking something for nothing. Even when successful, getting something for nothing destroys the precious asset of self-reliance. That argument, I fear, may leave the average person cold. All his training convinces him that getting something for nothing is attractive, but what comes next should destroy that conviction.

While the average person is alert to every chance to get something for nothing, that alertness causes him to be mentally restricted. He becomes victimized by a moral blackout that also distorts his logic. A person caught in that trap cannot achieve his full potential, whereas the person who escapes it becomes outstanding. That is a real opportunity, and the person who avails himself of that opportunity is the one who makes greatest vocational and social progress. His activities consistently put him ahead of the crowd.

Therefore, even when a person does not get what he seeks, the person who seeks something for nothing pays a higher price than the person who pays the proper price.

In the sense we are using the term, there is no such thing as a person with inferior mentality. Perhaps a person who has wrestled with a dull child is puzzled by that remark, but this book deals with the faculty that permits distinction between right and wrong. Everybody has that faculty, and I have found that it is a most vital aid to intelligence. By developing and exercising that faculty, a person markedly improves his intelligence. As a student my IQ was 105, whereas twenty years later, my test scores were in the top one percentile of the population.

Among average persons, there are no dullards. There are only some who have consigned themselves to dullness by their dishonest thoughts. They use dishonest means to seek advantage in relation to other people and often to blind themselves to their own shortcomings. They think that advantage is genuine, but I shall explain why it is counterfeit.

Perhaps you have encountered average persons who behave so stupidly that you wonder why. The reason is that they do not use their faculty to distinguish right from wrong. Instead, they habitually favor themselves and their interests in their thinking, and that causes them to favor their pocketbooks and their images. "But everybody does that," a person may say. "It's normal." Perhaps so, but it isn't right and should not be thought normal.

The habitually dishonest person bases much of his thinking on false premises, and to that extent, his conclusions are wrong. When a conclusion backfires, he may adjust it into more acceptable form in an effort to preserve his distorted illusion that he is right. So far as his private thinking is concerned, that is like cheating at solitaire. When welfare of others is involved, it is more like cheating at bridge. In any case it is dishonest, and because it is dishonest, it is wrong; and because it is wrong, it gets wrong results.

The dishonest person is a menace to everybody except to the person who lives by the principle of absolute right.

Most of all, the dishonest person is a menace to himself as his continued dishonest thinking keeps his thinking apart from reality.

Once I visited a scientific chicken farm and was taken into a building that housed thousands of chicks. Each chick wore a pair of tiny red spectacles. The manager explained, "Every chick will peck at a spot of blood," he said. "Soon the bloody chick will be dead. Without those glasses, the slightest injury is fatal."

We entered another building illuminated by red lights. "In this light," he said, "we are hoping to get the same effect at less cost."

The habitually dishonest person is like the chick in red spectacles. He cannot see whatever things his particular brand of dishonesty conceals. He is blind to certain of his mistakes, and also to certain of his opportunities. Since every decision he makes is missing a few vital facts, it is not surprising that his behavior often looks stupid to someone else.

He is not stupid. He is morally handicapped. And that is true whether his dishonesty is intentional or not.

While such persons are like chicks with red glasses, the world we live in is more like the second chicken house. People figuratively live under colored lights that tend to blind them to dishonesty. There are almost universal practices of dishonesty that are taught to children, used openly among adults and often pointed to as practical, diplomatic and good business. Small wonder if most people adopt those dishonest practices. Small wonder if society has problems it cannot solve.

Among all the people I have known, few were genuinely stupid, but there were many whose dishonesty had thrown their minds off the track and afflicted them with mental dullness.

Think about some stupid performance of a person you

know. Ask, "Isn't that a kind of trouble he could easily have avoided?" *What causes trouble for a person is less a lack of intelligence than a lack of honest thought.*

Those mental blinders are removed simply by applying the principle of absolute right. Then a person discovers that he is not stupified by the deceptive lights of dishonesty.

Over the years I have watched an occasional executive solve a new and perplexing problem without confusion or disaster. I watched as he streamlined and systematized the procedure so that it became easy to teach. Finally I watched him spend months trying to train another person who only awkwardly carried out the routine. Often the trainee was intelligent and educated, but the difference was in the degree of his moral blindness more than anything else.

From one year to the next, the average person never utters a profound thought unless he is quoting someone. He seldom displays real initiative or creative ability, because he does not use good tools of thought. He has those tools, but their value is canceled by his dishonesty. His ingenuity is consumed in efforts to create false favorable impressions and to hide impressions to his discredit. That is why dishonest advantage demands more ingenuity than honest success. When the average person unshackles his mind of its dishonesty, he makes various illuminating discoveries.

It may be true that honesty by itself is not a touchstone of success, but honesty releases a person's creative ability and gives it a right direction. Creative ability with wrong direction enables him dishonestly to contrive and protect a lie. Whether the lie is thought, stated or lived, its result is always wrong.

The individual who cleanses himself of dishonesty and wrong thinking thereby releases use of higher faculties. The person who fails to cleanse himself, to that extent, works against himself.

Wrongdoing results from wrong thinking. Wrong thinking leads to wrong words and wrong action. Nonetheless, the average person has an instinctive desire to be right. He wants to be known as right by others, but, above all, he wants to feel he is right in the recesses of his own conscience. So strong is this natural desire that he cannot do what is wrong without first convincing himself that the wrong is somehow right. He justifies it often by resorting to extremes of fantasy. The more of that sort of thinking he does, the more he mixes wrong information with right data in his ordinary thought processes.

The exception is the person who listens to reason, who admits wrongness the moment it is brought to his attention, who is diligent about finding his mistakes on his own account, and who never advances or defends what is wrong. He is a person worth knowing and one who bears watching. When given an opportunity, he handles it well. When given an obligation, he discharges it conscientiously. He finds satisfactory solutions to problems as they come along.

Part III

Rewards Are Beyond Ordinary Belief

Chapter 12

Temptations to Wrong Thinking

PRECEDING CHAPTERS have cited many examples of individual dishonesty, but there is an unfortunate thing about an example. It has the effect of associating the discussion only with the specific situation described. Even after the point is abundantly proved, people say, "Well, I guess you are right about the dishonesty in that incident, but what about other incidents?" The fact is that if they were all analyzed, it would be discovered that dishonesties were present in all of them.

In discussing the incentives to dishonest, wrong thinking with its consequent wrong words and wrong action, consider the following:

First, there is a kind of dishonesty so prevalent nobody can shrug it off—lying. Within the definitions of Chapter 8, lying is certainly as wrong as stealing, and each is entirely wrong. One kind of lying is as wrong as any other kind, for the same reason. The average parent does not want his children to lie any more than he wants them to steal, but the average parent does both when confronted with enough temptation.

If you ever operated a laundry, you would find that lost articles were generally bought last week and were very expensive. "Nobody ever loses anything old or cheap," a laundry owner once complained. His remark shows that lying and stealing are often two forms of the same thing, and it refers to a sort of trouble that burdens more people than laundry owners.

Every person who settles disputes, interviews applicants for employment, listens to personal appeals or stories told by people seeking opportunities of any sort knows that it is wise to look behind a speaker's words for the real truth. Unless the interviewer is well acquainted with the petitioner and has confidence in him, he knows the story virtually always is slanted in the petitioner's favor. It is calculated to credit him or her with wisdom, knowledge, ability or experience, popularly known as "selling yourself."

The astute listener can detect conversational dishonesty even on trivial subjects just by noticing facial expressions, gestures and physical posture. He can do it without even hearing the spoken words. The fact is that when personal interests are heavily involved, more conversations are dishonest than honest.

Most executives I have known so habitually make allowances for conversational dishonesty that, although they do not always know it, they become cynical. The executive who accepts the average stranger's word on vital matters seldom remains an executive, and the successful executive knows this so well he may pass up promising opportunities just to be safe.

The practice of discounting conversation is so general that even the honest person must often prove his points or have them rejected. Seasoned employers instinctively do that sort of discounting, but why confine the practice to them? Most people do it, because they have learned that otherwise they may be embarrassed or hurt by accepting misinformation.

Conversational dishonesty is so prevalent that it is taken for granted—often not noticed. People become inured to conversational dishonesty by exposure to it in thousands of conversations, beginning in childhood. When it is noticed, it may be called exaggeration, which is a polite way of describing deviations from truth.

People need a term harsh enough to carry real opprobrium so that dishonest conversation is not overlooked and excused. They should call it what it is—lying, and realize that conversational dishonesty is as destructive to intelligence as any kind of dishonesty.

The basic temptation to dishonesty is the average person's desire to favor himself, his interests and ambitions in everything he thinks, says and does. He wants to present himself to advantage and get the maximum tangible and intangible rewards he can.

From infancy, a person is surrounded by people who take dishonest shortcuts in order to satisfy their urges. They do it automatically and unthinkingly from force of habit and example, without ever stopping to consider the damage their dishonesty may cause. The average child copies those dishonest examples because few other examples are set before him. Gradually his use of dishonest technique becomes as automatic as it is to his elders. He continues using it unless, somewhere along the line, he gets a shock that causes him to change.

There is no reason why he should not advance his interests if they are honest. By advancing them, he benefits both himself and society. He benefits neither himself nor society by basing any portion of his progress on dishonesty. Best results develop if he realistically and honestly looks at life and its problems, knowing that unless he does, vital portions of his intelligence are rendered impotent.

There is only one way to be realistic: Deal in terms of absolute honesty and absolute right. I didn't make the rule, I can't change it and neither can anybody else because the rule exists in nature.

Absolute refusal to lie keeps a person out of situations that later may seem to call for a lie. For example, he is less likely to exceed speed limits when driving his car once he has denied himself lying as a way out if he is challenged. Refusal to lie is one of the things that puts people on the path of right and keeps them there.

Similarly his refusal to exaggerate compels him to develop his talents and to act responsibly, making exaggeration unnecessary.

At first, perhaps that makes things more difficult. If he has been operating on partial dishonesty, he loses that option. He is like a reformed counterfeiter who decides to spend only genuine money which means he then has to get a job. At first, the change seems a sacrifice, but one change is pure gain. When he eliminates the dishonest money-making, unless his past catches up to him, he ends all the risk that goes with counterfeiting. That relief soon compensates for any temporary sacrifice.

There is another difficulty that results from a switch to absolute honesty. Since people live in a dishonest society, most people cannot imagine that another person is genuinely honest. After people discount what they consider to be exaggeration from his honest remarks, there may not be much left. I learned that by experience and, at first, it was discouraging. Later I learned a more important lesson: ***Honesty automatically develops abilities in the average person that he never knew existed.*** As his abilities develop, they establish him favorably in the minds of others.

Here is what the foregoing information means to the average person. If he is scrupulously honest in all his conversations, he finds himself tending to satisfy the principle of absolute right in all areas. But it pays to be alert, as temptations to dishonesty are frequent and strong, for reasons I shall describe.

Underlying every dishonest performance is one or more of these typical temptations: The desire to get one's way, to get something for nothing, to stay out of trouble, or the desire for competitive advantage or revenge. Temptation is increased in proportion to these factors: The size of the advantage to be gained, the opportunity to gain it without getting caught, and the force of example set by other people's dishonest practices.

Consider a hypothetical case. Suppose a person is given the chance to secure enormous dishonest wealth. Suppose the wealth would enable him to prevent or correct serious trouble, free him from heavy responsibilities, enable him definitively to defeat his competitors and enemies. Suppose the opportunity for those ill-gotten gains is thrust upon him so that nobody will ever uncover the dishonesty involved and that it is the sort nearly everybody uses every day. How many people would refuse that temptation? How many would gleefully decide the millennium had arrived?

There is something wrong with that picture. The wealth to be gained is dishonest which means that it would cost more than it is worth. ***Honesty is priceless.*** Some people would object to that statement and consider the foregoing case to involve gain without loss. Does it? No!

For one thing it involves loss of integrity. I am not naive enough to believe that the average dishonest person puts a high value on integrity, so the prospect of losing integrity is a weak deterrent. Rather, he must feel threatened by something he wants.

The fact is that what a dishonest person sacrifices relates to his ability to think rationally. Would a person knowingly buy wealth at the price of his sanity? Only if he were already partly irrational at the time because of past dishonesties.

Something else is wrong with that picture.

The person who establishes his life on an honest basis acquires all the opportunities and possessions the dishonest person is tempted to pursue. As for wealth, he has all he needs. As for trouble, he is freed from it and in no danger of getting into more. As for responsibilities, he has those he wants, no more and no less. As for competitors, he has none. As for enemies, if he has any, they are persons trying to advance wrong causes. As for opportunities, he has an open road ahead with plenty of incentive to carry him forward. As to whether someone might publicize his actions, his life is an open book. As for temptation to dishonesty, he knows it points to danger. His intent always is to think, say and do what is right, and his reward is that whatever he does has a way of succeeding.

Safety experts have coined the term "accident prone." It indicates a person who has a history of frequent accidents, so judging by his history, he is the one most likely to have continuing accidents. Experience has demonstrated the term to be sound.

The next few paragraphs will develop the theory that the accident-prone person is usually suffering from habitual but perhaps unsuspected dishonesty. To the extent that such is the case, he is also dishonesty prone. That is not to say that every dishonesty-prone person is also accident prone; at least, not if you define an accident in the sense of physical injury or property damage.

But there are other kinds of accidents, and if you include them in your thinking, you will discover that the dishonesty-prone person is also accident prone in the precise fields of his dishonesty.

He gets into frequent arguments, finds it hard to win others' confidence, often loses their confidence once it is gained, habitually runs out of money, misses rides and appointments, has poor health, his coworkers gossip about him, he invites long runs of misfortune and blames his troubles on bad luck or other people.

A person needs to learn that virtually all trouble is pre-
ventable by the individual himself.

If readers do enough experimenting, they, too, will discover that the accident-prone person is also dishonesty prone
and that dishonesty is the root of the trouble. When a person
learns to be honest, he demonstrates the truth of what I have
said because his various accidents come to an end. I have
seen it happen to others, and it has happened to me.

While I cannot describe here the reasons why a person
is dishonesty prone, I can describe some of the types. They
will be recognized as typical of people everyone knows.

There is the person who is physically and mentally lazy.
Lacking proper motivation, he cannot meet his needs unless
he supplements his efforts with dishonest tactics. He is the
person who copies the original work of others and passes it
off as his own, who, literally and figuratively, blows his horn
to attract attention, or who seizes every dishonest advantage
that comes along.

The mentally lazy person, however, tends not to be very
dangerous. He does not use enough ingenuity to be dangerous in ways within the law. Therefore, he is less a threat than
the person whose dishonesty springs out of excessive ambition and the strong drives that ambition can generate.

If his conscience permits, the excessively ambitious person engages in every dishonest practice that helps to pro-
mote his plans. He seeks every means to perpetuate and
extend his power and resorts to unfairness to win the advantage. He tends to hurt his competitors, because he regards
them as enemies. He slanders them and assassinates their
reputations in an effort to undermine and block their
progress. His antisocial behavior is the product of his urges
which are measured against his standards of conduct. Where
no right standard prevails, his conscience is nonfunctional.

Perhaps nobody is more dangerously dishonest than the person who is strictly out for himself. He expresses his self-ish urges and tendencies until he is restrained by lack of opportunity, by force or until he is more compellingly restrained by enlightenment.

Next, there is the type of person who is dishonesty prone because he lacks a sense of responsibility. He doesn't exert his brain to make right decisions, and he doesn't exert his body to get things done right and prevent trouble. He doesn't correct the trouble he causes unless somehow forced. In a discussion he doesn't check the accuracy of his facts and rattles off nonsensical remarks with an air of authority. He is careless of other people's interests and welfare and perhaps also of his own.

There is the person who feels inferior; therefore, he tries to prove superiority. He uses every occasion to demonstrate his imagined qualities without understanding that every real quality expresses itself in his behavior more clearly than it is debated.

There is also the person whose mind is closed. He talks decisively about every topic among his special interests, and nobody can give him the correct information he needs because he has judged that he already knows it.

There is the person who is prejudiced. On those subjects, all his opinions reflect false premises that guarantee false conclusions.

There is the person who has to dominate every discussion. He blatantly varies his arguments to support whatever he is trying to prove.

Then there is the smart aleck who uses wisecracks and jokes to smother someone's sound opposition under laughter, capturing the attention of listeners who fall for his stratagem.

It becomes obvious that the dishonesty-prone person is the one who puts selfish desires above the intent to be right in what he thinks, says or does. He may try to gratify his desires often or seldom, but whenever he does, he exposes himself to trouble. He becomes vulnerable. To become invulnerable, a person needs only to adopt the intent to become right. Unless he has already done irrevocable damage, he can make that change in a flash by *deciding* to be right. However, he must live up to his decision, for he destroys his invulnerability every time he slips back into an old dishonest practice.

The sooner a person starts, the better for his body, soul, mind and general welfare. He makes no more sacrifice than the potential burglar who refrains from robbing a house. Anyone who considers that a sacrifice has changes to make in getting his thinking straightened out. So has the person who does not apply the principle of right action to dishonesty in every form.

The person who universally applies that principle discovers that his selfish desires begin to merge with what is right. *Invariably he discovers that what is right works and satisfies the need of every situation at the same time.* That is another basic principle known only to the honest person who intends to think, say and do what is right.

I think the foregoing demonstrates that masses of people are dishonest and that their dishonesty is the main cause of their troubles and of the world's troubles, too. There is no possibility of correcting those troubles until people correct the dishonesty that causes them.

Our next chapter will discuss a pernicious human tendency toward mass dishonesty that is almost never analyzed correctly so that support for it continues unabated.

Chapter 13

Exposing Organized Dishonesty

AT CERTAIN times and under certain conditions, various kinds of dishonesty become fashionable. The Prohibition era produced fashionable dishonesties of bootlegging, hijacking, gangsterism, speakeasies, bribery of officials, illegal distribution and use of alcoholic beverages. Wartime shortages produce the fashionable dishonesties of black markets, whereas peacetime shortages drive prices sky high on products already in stock and on the shelves.

Fashionable dishonesty arises when large numbers of people are simultaneously confronted with the same temptation. Those without conscience yield at once and get in on the ground floor. Those who originally demur, notice what is happening, and the less timid join the parade. Presently the person who still refrains begins feeling sorry for himself because he isn't getting his share, and he succumbs.

By that time the dishonesty has become so general that it would be impossible to jail all the offenders, even if the courts were so inclined. In any case the participants in that sort of dishonesty feel secure because mass dishonesty prevails.

Sometimes that sort of thing happens in a restricted area as when service men and women bring home loot from foreign countries and get their pictures published, not for their dishonesty but for their accomplishments.

Consider the false and misleading statements made to the citizenry during wartime by public officials. Because there is so much misinformation and because it is not fashionable to question it, most of their statements go unchallenged. But fashionable dishonesty is not confined to wartime nor is it always national in scope.

Consider an example of what is repeatedly observed by persons working in an industrial organization.

Any number of employees filch small items like paper, pens, stamps, pencils, and often materials and tools that are rather expensive. They know it is wrong, because they take great pains to conceal their thievery.

When caught, a person may defend the practice because it is so general that failure to do so seems like forfeiting a right. How far the trouble can go is suggested by the following case.

A company manufacturing radios discovered that its inventory was short by a quarter million dollars. After investigating, the company posted a notice which read: "Our parts inventory has recently dropped sharply. Investigation shows that company parts are being used to build radios at home. Hereafter, lunch boxes will be searched as employees leave. During the next thirty days where we have evidence that parts were stolen, homes will be searched." The notice added significantly, "No employees' lunch boxes will be searched on entering the plant."

Shortly a new inventory check disclosed that most of the missing parts had been returned to stock.

Next, I shall describe a somewhat complicated illustration that every industrial engineer will recognize as a common occurrence when opportunity arises.

Consider a company where production is handled on a piecework basis. Time-study men are employed to set the workers' rates. Often a worker intentionally delays a job while it is being measured. But those time-study men are experienced and allow for an amount of intentional delay.

Being human, however, they make mistakes. Consider a mistake that is typical.

A job is measured to include certain operations. One of the workers discovers a shortcut. Using that shortcut, he could turn out twice as many pieces, but he doesn't do that. Instead, he takes it easy. He turns out only half the number of extra pieces and makes extra money.

Time-study men learn that he is "running away with the rate." They watch him, but he conceals his actions. Unless they discover the shortcut and embody it in the manufacturing procedure, the union contract stipulates that the company may not alter the rate. The worker knows this, and that is why he keeps his shortcut to himself.

A fellow worker discovers the slick operator's secret and does the same thing. More and more operators get in on what they consider a good thing, and they conspire to protect their secret.

Some persons may think such things are common with laboring men, but I have spent much time with laboring men and have found them basically no different from other workers. The same sort of thing is often done where professionalism is usually assumed. Consider the profession of teaching.

To provide incentive for its teachers, a board of education established a new classification labeled "superior" teacher. The board set up the qualifications and announced that any teacher meeting them would receive a substantial pay increase. Those who could easily do so qualified at once. The others grumbled.

When any sort of extracurricular work was to be passed out, ordinary teachers got into the habit of saying, "Give that job to a superior teacher. I'm not good enough."

Many were less outspoken, but the superior teachers were soon earning their extra pay by doing all the extra work. The result? The board was forced to classify all teachers as superior regardless of their qualifications.

Those teachers changed the functioning of their economic unit, which is not unusual. Once a change becomes fixed, it is difficult or impossible to restore the original condition so that what starts as an abused privilege becomes a vested right.

Suppose a company announced that employees would be paid for periods of illness totalling thirty days a year. As many companies have discovered, that can lead to unexpected consequences.

Soon employees exert pressure to change the policy. Some arguments have enough logic that occasional exceptions are made. Each exception becomes a precedent. Before long, the company is forced to give everybody thirty free days each year in addition to his annual holidays and paid vacation. In addition, virtually every employee takes that time off whether he is sick or not.

The final result is that if an employee gets sick, he does it on his own time, because he has gained a vested interest in his extra time. From the viewpoint of this book, it is a dishonest system—which does not relate in any way to the merits or demerits of sick leave.

In describing those manifestations of fashionable dishonesty, I also described something that is known as the gravy train.

The mechanism is that one person sees another gain unfair advantage. He feels cheated, so, in seeking to right the wrong by imitating the dishonest procedure or finding a substitute, he takes the wrong step. Others see what is going on and join in. Soon a gravy train has formed. But note: No person gets on a gravy train unless he personally chooses to be dishonest.

The defense for such action is weak: Others are doing it,

and everybody is entitled to his share. Unfortunately, that weak defense often looks strong, because penalties cannot be applied on a mass basis. Life provides the penalties, but society cannot directly protect itself against mass dishonesty until each person learns to protect himself from himself. That takes a return to morality and to the properly functioning conscience.

Not being a candidate for public office, I intend to state what people often are afraid to say for publication.

Getting something for nothing, even when legal and fashionable, is dishonest. Getting too much for too little, even when the opportunity exists, is also dishonest. It is dishonest to seek that sort of gain and dishonest to accept it if successfully sought by others on your behalf. Having accepted it, it is dishonest to keep it.

It is evident that no gravy train is established out of love for its passengers. The purpose of the political gravy train is not to distribute gravy. It is to collect votes.

Let me repeat that the average person wants to do things right. He is convinced that he *is* right. Where he is shown that what he is doing is wrong, he changes. Few are willing to be wrong on purpose, especially when they are aware of what it costs them and others.

There is only one way to change a person from wrong to right: Bring his thinking into conformity with what is right. *When someone sees he is dishonest, that his dishonesty is visible to others, and that his dishonesty is costing him more than he is getting out of it, he changes.* Getting enough such people to change would wreck the various gravy trains.

Much trouble springs out of the fact that political leaders feel compelled to serve two masters: the party and the public. A national administration, in its desire to provide for the general good, must also keep a constant eye on the supporters who voted the party into power. To be more specific, the President is seldom free to have a differing opinion about matters of prime interest to the block of voters who got him elected and presumably can keep him there. On those matters, his thinking is likely to be adjusted to theirs. That kind of mental pressure is destructive to intelligence, no matter whose intelligence is involved.

. To a considerable extent, society is expected to live by dishonest techniques. Over the generations, those dishonest techniques have been refined and taught. Masses of people have discovered that they get results so do not question their honesty.

It may be true that people were as dishonest in earlier generations, but only this generation has had enough ingenuity to develop such an organized network of dishonest techniques that our dishonesty is finally at a point of engulfing us.

People should be reminded that there are plenty of honest techniques. Those honest techniques achieve more than dishonest techniques can achieve. *A small proportion of people using honest techniques can defeat a large proportion who do not.* There are people who already know this and are putting their knowledge to good use. What we need is millions more. When we have them, no political party would dare advance a program of pandering to individual or mass dishonesty for petty reward. *No honest person would be willing to sacrifice his integrity when he understands how a dishonest mess of pottage keeps him from his natural birthright.*

Chapter 14

How Fear Really Is Conquered

SOCIETY IS groping for something to help people out of their present crises. There is increasing recognition in numerous newspaper and magazine articles that we need mental, emotional and spiritual rebirth. Virtually any intelligent private or televised discussion of national or international affairs refers to the need for moral choices. You hear it from Republicans and Democrats, people in eastern Europe, the Soviet Union, and the Middle East, from leaders in high positions and low. It is slowly but surely penetrating the public's consciousness.

This book is issued to help that movement along.

In the foregoing pages, I made a number of strong assertions. For example, I asserted that *complete honesty makes the individual invulnerable, causes his life to open before him, confronts him with unending opportunities and constructive plans, and rightfully crowns his efforts with success.* I said, virtually all of life's problems are solved by simple and obvious choices between right and wrong. When those choices are honestly made by a majority of people, most troubles will cease. One troublesome situation after another could finally be resolved by resort to the principle of absolute right: *Think, say and do what is right; refuse to think, say and do what is wrong.*

This nation affords an excellent social climate in which broadscale honesty can thrive. Americans are favored with freedom that, more than anything else, provides the opportunity to choose right instead of wrong. We have opportunities in abundance that should be intelligently shared. *Americans are confronted with economic and career opportunities that have never existed. They have every incentive to make the most of those opportunities, and the way to do it is honestly to think, say and do what is right.* It is often argued that society needs more and better laws. Personally, I do not agree, and I disagree with the popular assumption that we cannot legislate morality. On the other hand, I'd rather not live in a society where nobody can make a decision without consulting a lawyer nor among people who need such laws. I want to live among people who are trying to do what is right and who are not penalized if they make a well-intentioned mistake. Their wrong result would guide their minds back to the right track.

In the final analysis, honesty is an individual matter. Each person must individually decide to make his own choices between right and wrong.

However, the results of dishonesty are more than individual in scope. When masses of people make wrong decisions, especially when wrong decisions are made by public officials, the effect is devastating indeed. When group dishonesty shapes national thinking, it causes national and international conflict and injustice. Even when we do not realize it, group dishonesty has a way of injuring people where it hurts the most. *When people realize that group dishonesty causes national and international troubles, those troubles can be corrected.* There is only one way to do that—correct individual dishonesty. The most influential individuals to reach are those in positions of strategic leadership, but everybody is important.

Each individual doing what he knows is right and

refusing to do what he knows is wrong ensures a secure future. Let him do it in his vocational, public and private life. That is *the* way to solve our local, national and international problems. At the time of this writing, it has never been tried on a broad scale.

Because the absolutely right way of life has been almost entirely rejected, society lives in fear.

In modern times, no generation has been so anxious, so frightened, so confused. People are afraid of war, economic recession, ecological disruption, fuel shortages, racial injustices and so on. Most of their fears are misdirected.

A twelve-year-old boy said to his mother, "You know, Mom, I wish I were forty years old."

"Whatever gave you that idea?"

"Because I heard that everybody will be killed when the bombs go off. If I were over forty, I'd have had my life, and I wouldn't care!"

Do you fear nuclear destruction? I don't. The reason is partly that I cannot control use of the bombs. Since fear is nature's prod for stimulating constructive action, that makes fearing it nonproductive, but there is a deeper reason.

Nuclear weapons are dangerous only if handled irresponsibly; they are dangerous if exploded in our midst—by an enemy or accidentally by us. Natural fear would be directed at the enemy or the military rather than the bomb, and that is a fear we can do something about.

Fear of nuclear weaponry is really fear of the political and military leaders having it. It is fear of how those leaders may deal with one another. Despite any futility a person may feel, that is something he can influence.

It is done by making certain that every decision he makes is an honest decision to take and support right action.

I once heard an ex-congressman address a large gathering of industrial executives. He discussed the shortcomings of our government and said our government is riddled with dishonesty and corruption. No person in the audience tried to deny it.

Our government, according to that ex-congressman, is spending its way into bankruptcy, reelecting itself by promising unearned handouts, crippling industry by taxation, socializing us beyond our means, sapping the self-reliance of individual citizens by training them to depend on government, and otherwise progressively undermining the American system of free enterprise.

There is no need to identify that ex-congressman. I had heard the same speech thirty times before, idea for idea, though not word for word. Every such talk elicited thunderous applause; never did any listener raise a word of dissent.

Do you fear those conditions that ex-congressman described? I don't, and the reason is that I cannot control those conditions. Again, that makes fearing them nonproductive. But insofar as the assertions are justified, I fear the persons who caused them. And that is also a fear people can do something about.

Each person does his part by basing every decision on an honest decision to live by the principle of absolute right.

Many important problems beset society. It is common knowledge that there is corruption in our national, state and local governments. Every dishonest decision a person makes gives his tacit support to rackets, graft and dishonest leadership. *What is needed is a majority of persons who habitually distinguish between right and wrong and use their consciences to move in the direction of right.* Those people will improve their lives at once, and when there are enough of them, society will be led into unimagined national and international peace and prosperity.

Once I rode downtown with another driver. I was in no hurry, but the driver was. Suddenly he saw a chance to save two seconds by squeezing between two fast-moving cars. "That was tight," I said.

"Was it?"

"Didn't you see it?" I asked.

"No," said the driver. "When I see a tight squeeze coming, I close my eyes."

Needless to say, that was my last ride with that driver.

Whether we like it nor not, we are being taken for the same sort of ride every day of our lives by irresponsible and dishonest local, state and national leaders who were not trained to develop personal integrity of the sort demanded by life.

There is no use ignoring the situation, we face many crises. Our leaders are constantly squeezing through tight places, taking corners on two wheels, blindly screeching through dilemmas, and encountering potential disaster. They are doing the driving, and we are passengers who can't get out.

Consider another figure of speech.

Society is sitting on a pile of nuclear bombs while sinister strangers finger the trigger mechanism. People are struggling toward financial security while inflationary forces and "deficit drain" suck the wealth out of their incomes and savings. People are trying to succeed under the free enterprise system while fuzzy-minded radicals use acts of terror and threats of war to meddle with that form of government. People are trying to vote intelligently while dishonest politicians sacrifice the public's future welfare to favor their own political ambitions.

There is no sense pretending that such things are not happening. To ignore them is to emulate the proverbial ostrich and hide our heads in the sand. There also is no sense in thinking nothing can be done about it either. Something can be done.

What, precisely, is being done?

Our leaders are making emphatic statements and accusations to those people who already agree with them. That is as much as most leaders are doing. Most other people, as a matter of fact, are doing much less. They are taking mental sedatives: watching television, following the sports news, going to vacation spots, conducting business as usual, fiddling while Rome burns. To quiet their fears, other people turn to literary sedatives: learning to cultivate happiness, overcome fear, be number one and acquire excellence along with peace of mind.

By reading books that tell readers how to be happy despite society's troubles, the public is trying to relieve a national anxiety complex. Those books are not relieving the anxiety. Society needs something more in the nature of a purgative; it needs a turn to honesty.

The trend toward mental sedatives is understandable. In the face of local, national and world conditions that are so tense and potentially volatile, it seems a relief to be diverted by fantasies and comic offerings of the entertainment world.

People can read "how to" books, apply them and go on suffering—unless they face up to one basic fact. *The fact is that peace, constructive action and prosperity develop as the result of thinking, saying and doing what is right.*

There is an unfortunate effect about the peace-of-mind approach to life. It is not dynamic. It palliates instead of energizing. This is an age for progress if ever there was one. Besides, people do not really want mental and emotional ease. People are built for action. They crave excitement. Watch them on the highway, at the race track, cheering sports' events, doing action things that are intended to stimulate the good life.

While the average person may think he wants mental and

physical rest, what happens when he gets it? He is bored. He looks for something to do. He wants action. Most of all, he enjoys the thrill of achievement.

Akin to the desire for peace of mind is the average person's passionate desire for happiness. That, too, is overestimated. The thoughtful person understands that happiness loses significance when it is bought by appeasement of an unprincipled person or any other compromise.

The average person may cringe because he generates emotional tensions of fear and unhappiness. But all tensions are not negative. There are constructive tensions. *A constructive tension is an emotional force to be used for constructive action. It can be considered an unsatisfied drive toward a right result.* If people seek artificial means of relieving those tensions, they lose their stimulus and value. By learning the knack, negative tensions can be relieved by simply giving effective expression to constructive action. Tensions could be compared to a tightly wound clock spring that releases its stored-up energy in useful work.

In the final analysis it will be discovered that constructive tensions result from honesty and negative tensions result from dishonesty. There is an easy way to build constructive tensions, and the same expedient converts negative tensions: Conform with the principle of absolute right. *Think, say and do what is right; refuse to think, say and do what is wrong.*

The person who applies that principle of behavior finds that his tensions drive him to choose right instead of wrong. He achieves invulnerability and an exciting, new way of life.

Such a person conquers every fear.

For purposes of this book, fear can be divided into two general categories. First is fear that arises from the individual's own sense of personal inadequacy as when he feels unequal to his problems. Second is fear that springs out of social conditions that loom threateningly as when the cards of life seem to be stacked against him.

There is a single procedure for overcoming both those fears. It happens when the individual exerts himself to do what is right. The more resistance he encounters in himself, the greater the opportunity to develop physical, emotional and mental power. The very conditions that engender fear provide a challenge. It is intelligent to meet that challenge rather than to accept defeat. *Start taking right action and fear diminishes. Keep moving in the right direction and fear dissolves.*

The person whose life is based on taking steps to satisfy right objectives experiences periodic peaks of great happiness. That happiness provides enough satisfaction to keep him safely exhilarated, although there is also enough natural dissatisfaction to keep him surging ahead.

With every forward step, he adds to his capacity for happiness. He overcomes fear. He learns that fear springs only from failure to deal with the situations of life. He learns that the person who accepts the demands of life without rebelling is too busy to be afraid. He also learns that running from those demands generates fears he cannot vanquish.

The way to conquer fear is to deal with every situation in complete honesty. Each constructive step reduces boredom and generates enthusiasm for the next. The person who takes an unending series of constructive steps has intervals of rest and diversion that give him happiness and deep satisfaction. Those intervals only recur as he continues inviting them by thinking, saying and doing what is right.

I have been discussing the essential objective of honest, right action. No matter how discouraged a person feels, he can boost his spirits by helping that cause along. Each time he adds an impulse to the cause for right action, he gets the thrill of a good job well done.

Perhaps a reader might still be inclined to question, "What can I do?"

I suggest that he or she recognize the challenge of today's world and meet life head on. Square himself with his conscience. Do what he can to improve conditions. See that every personal decision is completely honest. If a person does that, he can face the future unafraid. He does it by waging an intentional campaign of aggressive honesty. Nobody can do it by following the commonplace custom of pretending that problems don't exist or that there is nothing to be done about them.

I have stated again and again that *a life lived in accord with the principle of absolute right will be a life of satisfaction and achievement.* That is true. *The person who lives such a life benefits everybody on earth. He will benefit posterity. Before he benefits anyone else, he benefits himself, because he has a dynamic formula for successful accomplishment.* It is a fortunate fact that the formula is not open to abuse. He cannot cause trouble for other people nor for himself by using it. Neglecting to use the formula is what causes trouble for them and for him.

Virtually every religion teaches that present in our universe there are two basic opposing forces. They are the forces of good and evil. Those forces are symbolically expressive of God and Satan. It is the good force that causes people to follow the right path, and it is the evil force that causes them to follow the wrong path.

Whether a person accepts the religious explanation or not, it should be clear that every right choice releases a force for good, whereas every wrong choice releases a force for evil. The choice of wrong thoughts, words and action results in trouble, but the consistent choice of right thoughts, words and action results in unlimited benefits for the person, his countrymen and the people of the world.

It is worth something to recognize that what is wrong in life is based on emotional unreality and is temporary. What is right in life is part of the reality that unfailingly endures, establishing the principle that right is might.

Appendix

Summation of Fundamental Concepts

Chapter 11: *The Great Cost of Being Wrong*

Chapter 12: *Temptations to Wrong Thinking* Page

Chapter 13: *Exposing Organized Dishonesty* Page

Chapter 14: *How Fear Really Is Conquered*   Page